ANDREA GHISOTTI

FISH
OF THE
MALDIVES

340 Illustrations

All the marine species illustrated
in this book were
photographed by the author
in their natural habitat

BONECHI

SUMMARY

KEY

*The following graphic scheme is used for
the scientific nomenclature in the text:*

> **PHYLUM**
> Class
> *Subclass*
> ORDER
> **Family**

FISH OF THE MALDIVES

Projet: Casa Editrice Bonechi
Publication manager: Monica Bonechi
Artwork and video lay-out: Maria Rosanna Malagrinò

Photos, text and captions: Andrea Ghisotti
Editing: Simonetta Giorgi *and* Patrizia Fabbri

Translation: Kate Willcock

Map: Studio Grafico Daniela Mariani-Pistoia

E-mail:bonechi@bonechi.it
Internet:www.bonechi.it

ISBN 88-8029-657-4

* * *

Introduction

If the Red Sea is felt by us Europeans to be our "home sea", just round the corner from us, the Maldives are a dreamed of aspiration, a tropical paradise where time stands still, rising in the middle of the Indian Ocean. The arrival by aeroplane is in itself a stirring experience: the last minutes in the air unfolding the incredible prospect from above of atolls, little islands, ribbons of white sand and lagoons of matchless beauty, followed by landing on a runway which ends a few metres from a crystal-clear sea. The travellers get into dhonies, the beautiful and gracile Maldivian boats and the holiday begins at once, sailing on cobalt-coloured water towards their chosen island

destination, or to the chartered craft which will take them on an unforgettable cruise round the atolls. Male, the lively capital, rich in trade, in bell-ringing bicycles, mopeds and cars, is the only city in the Maldives. It is the only place where there are mechanics' workshops, wood merchants, shops brimming over with spices and grains, dried and fresh fish, ironmongers, fruit and vegetable merchants, shark fins and jaws, restaurants full of curry and umpteen boutiques and souvenir shops for tourists. But nobody comes to the Maldives to stay in the capital, it is conceded a brief visit at the

start or end of one's holiday. The rest is sea and peace on small and quiet islands, cloaked in palms and mangroves, with ribbons of the finest sand lapped by water which is always warm and is teeming with life. A mask

and fins suffice to discover the marvellous colours of fish, corals, shellfish, gorgonians, turtles and thousands of other animals which live a few metres from the shore.
This book provides the enthusiast with a practical guide to the fauna of the Maldives, and is intended to help identification of the more common species. In order to make recognition easier, every

species is illustrated with one or more photographs taken exclusively underwater of living subjects and accompanied by a simple but scientifically correct text which describes the particular characteristics of each group. Each photograph is accompanied by the Latin name of the species or animal which though it may seem unnecessarily complicated is actually the only official language of science.

3

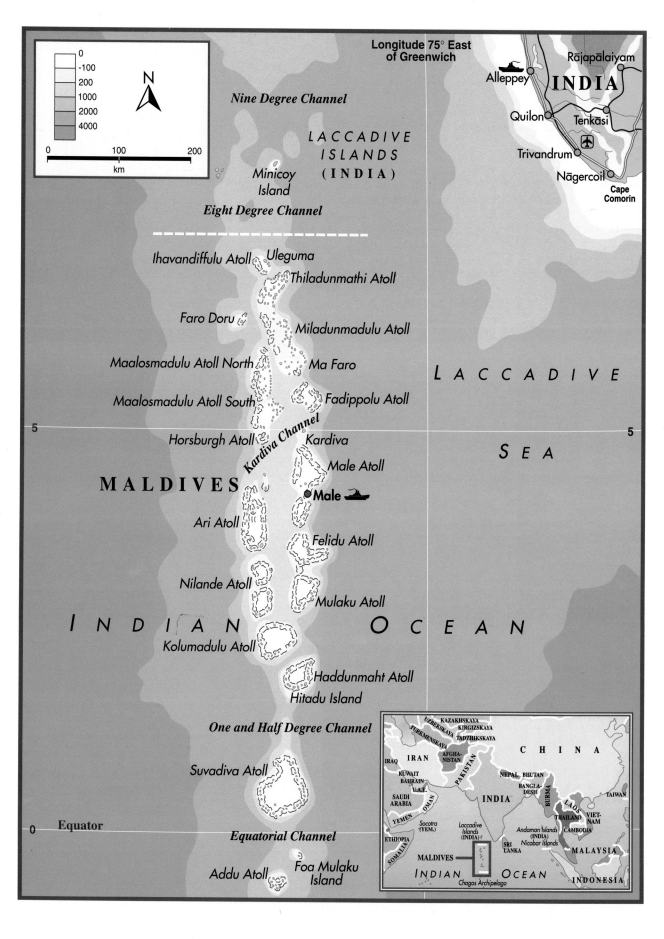

Longitude 75° East
of Greenwich

Nine Degree Channel

L A C C A D I V E
I S L A N D S
(I N D I A)

Minicoy
Island

Eight Degree Channel

Ihavandiffulu Atoll Uleguma

Thiladunmathi Atoll

Faro Doru

Miladunmadulu Atoll

Maalosmadulu Atoll North *Ma Faro*

Maalosmadulu Atoll South *Fadippolu Atoll*

5

Horsburgh Atoll *Kardiva*

Kardiva Channel

M A L D I V E S *Male Atoll*

Male

Ari Atoll

Felidu Atoll

Nilande Atoll

Mulaku Atoll

I N D I A N

Kolumadulu Atoll

Haddunmaht Atoll

Hitadu Island

One and Half Degree Channel

Suvadiva Atoll

0 Equator

Equatorial Channel

Addu Atoll *Foa Mulaku Island*

L A C C A D I V E

S E A

O C E A N

INDIA

Alleppey Rājapālaiyam

Quilon Tenkāsi

Trivandrum

Nāgercoil
Cape
Comorin

0
-100
200
1000
2000
4000

N

0 100 200
km

KAZAKHSKAYA
UZBEKSKAYA KIRGIZSKAYA
TURKMENSKAYA TADZHIKSKAYA
IRAQ IRAN AFGHA- CHINA
NISTAN
KUWAIT PAKISTAN NEPAL BHUTAN
BAHRAIN
SAUDI U.A.E. BANGLA-
ARABIA OMAN INDIA DESH BURMA TAIWAN
YEMEN LAOS
Socotra THAILAND VIET-
ETHIOPIA (YEM.) Laccadive NAM
Islands CAMBODIA
SOMALIA (INDIA) Andaman Islands
SRI (INDIA) MALAYSIA
LANKA Nicobar Islands
MALDIVES
I N D I A N O C E A N INDONESIA
Chagos Archipelago

THE MALDIVES

The archipelago of the Maldives is made up of 1190 islands which are strung out like pearls in a long necklace, in the Indian Ocean, about 700 kilometres south-west of Sri Lanka. The islands lie on a rocky ridge which rises from the bottom of the ocean at 4000 metres to a depth of around 70 metres, and they are grouped in 26 main atolls, each of which is made up of dozens of islands, even though from an administrative point of view there are 19 atolls. The archipelago, which stretches between latitudes 7°07' N and 0°42' S for a total length of 754 kilometres and a maximum breadth of 188, actually has a very small surface area, of 298 square kilometres. Not many more than 200 of the islands are populated, and the others are totally uninhabited. The capital and centre for all commercial and administrative activity is Male, the only real city of the Maldives, even though it certainly bears very little resemblance to our overcrowded western megalopolises. Many buildings have coral walls, some roofs are still made of palm fronds and most of the roads are not asphalted but made with white coral sand. The activity of Male is based round the port, which is of vital importance for the Maldivian Republic, given that all goods arrive by sea, mostly from eastern countries, who over the years have taken on an important commercial role for the archipelago. Ships cannot enter the port because of the inadequate draught and they anchor off-shore, thus almost all the boats moored in the port are the splendid *dhonies*, the characteristic

Maldivian boats, built on the islands using ancient techniques. In contrast with usual boat construction techniques, in these boats the supporting structure is provided by planking and not by frames, a construction technique used by the ancient Greeks and the Phoenicians and then handed down to the Romans. Their shape is narrow and tapering, with a smallish keel, in order to reduce their draught requirement considerably and allow them to sail in the shallow coastal lagoons. Previously the dhonies were sailing boats or, in an emergency, oars were used, but now they are equipped with Japanese motors which allow more reliable links and trade between the various islands and between these and the capital. Towards the evening the fishing dhonies arrive in the port of Male, loaded with little tuna fish, which with rice are the principal food source for the Maldivians. The catch is laid out on the floor of the fish market where it is purchased for individual consumption. For a small sum of money expert cutters will clean it, handing over fillets in 40-45 seconds, boned and skinned, a dance of blood and knife not to be missed. Not all the fish is taken, however, to Male, a large part remains on the islands for local consumption, where it is dried in the sun or smoked in special ovens.

The island economy is based above all on fish, the coconut harvest and on a bit of agriculture, carried out almost exclusively by the women. Life goes on peacefully and rarely is the authority of the head of the village called upon

The typical appearance of these islands, low-lying on the water and covered with luxuriant vegetation.

to settle controversies, given that the people are of a very peaceable disposition: it is unusual to hear so much as a raised voice here, let alone an argument. The authority of the head of the village is in other ways considerable given that the islands have a rather autarkic and largely autonomous form of government, especially those furthest away from the capital, from which several days sailing are required to reach it.

Tourism arrived in this remote world gradually and imperceptibly from the start of the '70s, with the first airline flights landing on the runway constructed on Hulule, an island a few minutes by boat from the capital. Then the airport was composed of a wooden shed and each visitor was allotted a progressive number. Subsequently the runway was lengthened to allow huge jumbos packed full of tourists to land. Very soon the first spartan bungalows gave way to comfortable villages, mostly, however, constructed with a certain taste and with extensive use of coral rock and wood. Today there are around eighty tourist villages, most of which are concentrated on the atolls of North Male, South Male and Ari, and can be reached from the airport of Hulule by dhonies in half an hour more or less for those dotted around near the capital and up to 4 hours for the more distant ones. The last few years have seen

the introduction of fast motor boats in order to shorten the longer journeys and some islands are also connected via helicopter with the airport. There is an overwhelming contrast between life in the tourist villages and that of the local people. Right from the start, the government passed laws to protect the marine environment, prohibiting underwater fishing and shell and coral collection everywhere, but without a doubt, the influence that such very different cultures and habits may have on the local population raises fears for the integrity of the country. For this reason tourist access is limited to the five atolls nearest the capital and even on the islands which have tourist villages there are zones reserved for Maldivians where tourists are debarred. In the last few years another type of tourism, as opposed to that of the villages, has developed: cruises, one or two weeks long, on board special charter boats. These boats are built on the islands and are structured on the waterlines of the dhonies but are built on a considerably larger scale with superstructures suitable to comfortably accommodate ten or so tourists. This is the most pleasurable way to visit these enchanted islands as the sea inside the atolls is almost always calm and one can visit remote islands and sleep in uncontaminated corners of paradise.

THE MALDIVIAN ATOLLS

The Maldives can only be reached by aeroplane, thus before landing, all tourists see the breathtaking aerial panorama: a continuous necklace of atolls with the stupendous turquoise colouring of the shoals and the coral reefs which encircle the islands contrasting with the surrounding sea of a deeper blue due to its greater depth.

On the formation of the atolls and islands two main theories have been advanced, which even today still cause debate between experts. The starting point of both is an indispensable condition for the growth of coral, that of finding itself in water shallow enough for sunlight to penetrate. This allows chlorophyll synthesis and thus permits the development of unicellular algae which live in symbiosis with the corals and seem to be very important for their growth.

The first theory is attributed to Darwin and is called "the theory of subsidence". The English scientist maintained that the origin of an atoll was an island produced by volcanic activity round which a first coastal barrier reef formed. Subsequently the island starts to sink, but as the nature of coral allows the birth and growth of new coral on old dead coral, gradually an external circular barrier is formed, with a shallow internal lagoon and an island at the centre of the lagoon, the remains of the primitive volcanic island. This may then continue to sink, eventually disappearing entirely and thus allowing the formation of the typical circular atolls with no central island.

The theory advanced by Daly in 1919, on the other hand, is based on the change in sea level during glaciation. When huge masses of ice form, the sea level goes down and certain parts of the sea bottom may emerge out of the water or in any case be much nearer the surface, allowing the development of coral formations. When afterwards, during the interglacial periods, the sea level starts to rise progressively, coral growth continues, forming barrier reefs and atolls, without for this reason making volcanic activity and subsequent sinking of an island necessary.

What really happened is probably a combination of the two theories, even if in the case of the Maldives, Daly's theory seems very probable since the archipelago is positioned on a rocky ridge which from 4000 metres rises to 70 metres from the surface, the peaks of which probably emerged during the last glaciation. At all events, the merit for such beauty is due to the minute coral polyps which are able to extract calcium carbonate from the water, with which they build their own skeleton. Onto these, other calcareous strata are superimposed building up, over a few million years, the great coral formations.

Single colonies can reach huge dimensions and an incredible quantity of forms: spherical, in columns, fan-shaped or branched in the most varied and fantastic ways. Even the colours are full of variety ranging from yellow to pink, from green to purple, from brown to blue. The colouring lasts as long as the corals are alive, after death they loose the surface tissue and only the white calcareous skeletons remain, dotted with the little holes where the polyps lived. These are the living part of the great colonies. Each polyp looks like a little contractile sac with an annular crown of tentacles arranged round an opening which acts as a mouth. The tentacles have stinging cells which eject a filament similar to an arrow and a toxin capable of stunning small prey like the microscopic planktonic shell fish on which the polyps feed.

Other organisms able to secrete calcareous substances, like "fire-corals" and many species of "coral-algae" which are all-important in the building of the coral formations due to their cementing function, contribute to the construction of the reefs.

The great coral reefs are usually to be found in shallow waters, only rarely as deep as 100 metres; furthermore they require warm water (between 20°C - 68°F - and 35°C - 96°F) and cannot tolerate low salinity or very turbid waters.

A small island with white sand and a dense palm-grove is all that shows above water of a much more extensive submerged reef.

a

DANGEROUS

There are very few dangerous animals in the Maldives and incidents are rare. The much feared **sharks** (a), for example, have never caused casualties despite the over a thousand dives which take place in these waters every day. Not that it is rare to see a shark, on the contrary, certain shoals are well known to offer an almost certain encounter with these fascinating predators. Seeing a shark, however, does not mean that it will approach and even less that it will attack. After an inspection tour they swim away again towards the open sea, disappearing out of sight very fast. Although they possess considerable offensive powers, the sharks which one encounters in the Maldives practically never use them on divers, as long as their aggression is not unleashed by ridiculous offers of food or provocative or risky behaviour. Certain night dives in the passes should be avoided, as should also be the improvising of "circus" shows, offering fish, which could bring on a decidedly dangerous food-frenzy. Thus we can exclude the sharks which have a clear criminal record with respect to attacks on men in these waters, and concentrate on the organisms we should avoid. Among the fish the first place in the list must go to the **Scorpaenidae** (d) whose sting is positively dangerous. The members of this family are characterized by the presence of spines connected to poison glands positioned on the dorsal fin and often also on the pectoral fins. When these spines puncture the skin, an extremely potent neurotoxin is injected which causes unbearable shooting pains, local swelling, sweating, respiratory problems, quickening of heart beat, fever and in some cases paralysis and even death. Because these are thermolabile poisons, the effects of which diminish with rise in temperature, the part of the body in question must be immersed in hot water, as hot as is bearable, as soon as possible and diluted oxidising agents, like potassium permanganate must be applied to fight the toxic effect of the poison; analeptics for the heart and adrenalin and cortisone must also be administered. Scorpionfish differ in appearance according to the species. The

b

c

ANIMALS

lionfish *(Pterois)* have very showy colouring and their dorsal and pectoral fins are feathery and striped so as to warn potential aggressors that they are dangerous. Fortunately they have a peaceable nature and problems may only arise if an inexperienced diver tries to touch them. A quite different case are the terrible **stonefish** *(Synanceia verrucosa)* and the big **Scorpaenidae** *(Scorpaenopsis sp.)* which

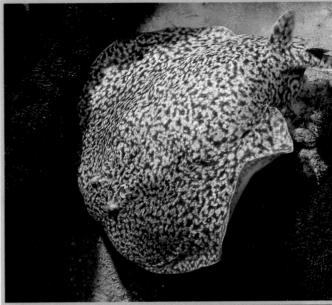

are incredibly mimetic and wait immobile on the reef or on the bottom for prey to come within their striking range. One may not always be aware of their presence, but danger is usually limited, given that divers should never rest on the reef, to avoid damaging it, and even less should they walk on it. Other animals armed with dangerous spines are the **stingrays** (f) which have a serrated aculeus which they use with great dexterity if necessary, driving it into the body of an aggressor. This again is, however, purely a defense weapon which the stingrays resort to using only if they believe themselves to be in danger. Divers are sometimes struck by their spine, but only if they bother them, touching them and trying to "play", behaviour which should be avoided with all aquatic animals as they can ill interpret our intentions and in any case risk being damaged by contact with our hands which rub off protective mucus and scales and thus favour infestation by parasites. The same is true of **moray eels** (c), which many divers and instructors like to stroke. Incidents have occurred and a good look at the moray eels' deadly set of teeth and reflection on their exceptional strength should suffice to convince one of the wisdom of the rule "look but don't touch". The big moray eels are always very peaceable, whilst certain small species which lurk in the crevices of the reef may bite even if not touched, especially

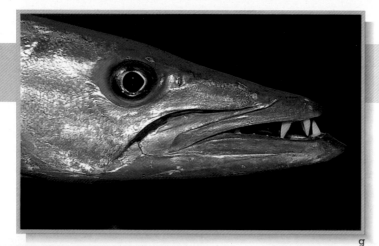
g

if a diver kneels down to take a photograph near their hole. Through a wet suit their bites are luckily not dangerous, but it is, however, worth the trouble to take care where one rests. Despite their threatening appearance and searching look, **barracudas** (g) do not attack divers, even when they group together in large shoals. Triggerfish may bite, on the other hand, particularly the big *balistoides viridescens* when it is guarding its eggs which are laid in large circular nests. If one goes too close it does not hesitate to attack and one must beat a hasty retreat to escape its courageous and determined action.

h

Contact with **electric rays** (e) is not dangerous though certainly "electrifying"; these are flat fish similar to rays and stingrays, endowed with sophisticated electric organs very like batteries, able, at the right moment, to discharge a potent electric shock to stun prey or frighten an aggressor. **Surgeonfish** (m) are endowed with laminated bone plaquettes on the sides of their tails which in some species are really sharp. Danger to divers is limited to those who try to catch them, in which case they can inflict deep and painful wounds.

The risk of invertebrates is mainly due to the stinging power of some species, a problem which can easily be resolved by wearing a wet suit complete with footwear and a pair of gloves, and above all, avoiding touching the reef. The stinging power of some **jellyfish** (h) is well known but they are not common in

i

the Maldivian waters whilst contact with certain **hydrozoans**, like the well known **fire-coral** (l), which looks like a mustard-coloured coral with white tips, is much more likely.

On contact with the skin a toxin is injected which causes unpleasant "burns" which must be treated with cortisone or aluminium sulfate cream. The same sort of burns are caused by **stinging sea-fan hydroids**, which look like white or yellowish little plants, and, in a milder way, by some sea **anemones** and certain **cnidaria**. The long spines of **diadem sea urchins**, which are mainly active at night, can easily penetrate the neoprene of the wet suit, breaking off in the flesh and causing intense pain, not so much because of the wound but due to a toxin contained in the thin epidermic layer covering the spines. Even the little spines which cover the arms of the **brittle stars** (i) can easily penetrate fingers where they remain deeply embedded in the flesh.

Finally, care should be taken with the beautiful **cone-shells** which can discharge real little harpoons connected to a poison gland. In some species present in the Maldives, such as the *Conus textile* and the *Conus geographus*, the poison is so potent that it can sometimes cause the death of the person who picked it up.

l

m

SNORKELLING AND SCUBA

All the tourist villages of the Maldives have a well equipped Diving Centre, which can be relied on to organise all underwater activities, both snorkelling and using an aqualung. The activity of pure observation, or snorkelling as it is called today, really is within the reach of anyone who is able to swim sufficiently safely and it requires very little equipment: a mask, a pair of fins and a snorkel. Ideally this equipment should be bought in one's own city where a reliable shopkeeper can advise on the choice of the models most fitted to one's needs. Fins should preferably be the closed shoe type, that is without straps and not too long, the mask must cling perfectly to the face and not allow water to enter, the snorkel should be soft and not uncomfortable even if used for long periods.

Contact with coral and other organisms can cause abrasions and grazes on the skin which can easily get infected in tropical climates, therefore it is advisable to wear a one-piece or two-piece wet suit of 3 mm thickness, or a lightweight lycra suit.

These garments also give good protection against unpleasant contact with stinging organisms and allow one to stay longer in the water by giving efficacious protection from the cold. The internal sea bottoms of the Maldivian reefs are very suitable for snorkelling, with a particularly rich fauna starting in the first metres of water, which permits even those who stay on the surface of the water to observe a good number of fish and invertebrates. Little dives under water enable one easily to approach many reef fish, whilst deeper dives may reserve wonderful surprises: if the snorkeller moves smoothly in the water without making abrupt movements, large pelagic creatures may be induced to draw near, full of curiosity.

Diving with compressed air cylinders is obviously even more exciting. On every island diving courses are organised and they allow anyone to reach an adequate mastery of the use of equipment and diving techniques in just a week, obtaining the relevant international certification. There are also even shorter courses, a kind of introduction to diving which allow one to try it without having to undertake a real course which inevitably involves theoretical knowledge with relative lessons.

The best thing is to arrive in the Maldives with one's certification already in one's pocket and some good diving experience, so as to fully enjoy the holiday period, diving right from the very first day. Dives take place almost exclusively from boats and thus require some experience of free water descent, without a reference point and the analogous re-ascent.

The biggest difficulty to be met with at the Maldives is due to the presence of currents which are often felt, and sometimes with such considerable intensity as might create problems. The boatmen and instructors are prepared to deal with it, but obviously single divers are required to have the necessary skill to manage in all situations, with good consumption monitoring and efficient use of the equilibrator jacket.

Only 10, 12 or 15 litre mono-cylinders are used and they almost always have single attachment taps and fittings, thus it is useless to bring two separate regulators, only one of which could be mounted.

More useful would be to have already prepared an "octopus" at home, that is a single first stage with two second stages. The temperature of the water is warm all year round, fluctuating between 27°C (80°F) and 29°C (84°F), therefore a one-piece or two-piece 3mm wet suit without a hood will more than suffice. The most suitable footwear is that with rigid soles which allow one to walk quite safely in shallow water and which require the use of fins with straps. The equipment is completed with an equilibrator jacket, a knife, a pair of protective gloves and a torch to enable one to see into the numerous holes and crevices in the reef and which is indispensable for night dives.

Lastly, a computer is rather useful; it automatically calculates the absorption of nitrogen during each dive taking into account the nitrogen not yet eliminated from previous dives. This instrument is growing more and more widespread among divers and increases the pleasure and safety of diving.

UNDERWATER PHOTOGRAPHY

Whoever has the fortune to dive in the Maldivian seas will inevitably be overwhelmed by the wish to document and take home that incredible multicoloured world, even if only in the form of photographs and slides. To obtain good results is not, however, so easy and requires much more sophisticated and expensive equipment than the purchase of a little disposable waterproof camera. The optical and physical problems involved in taking taking pictures underwater require lenses of considerable definition and, above all, the use of a flash which cannot be incorporated into the camera given that in this way the large and small particles in suspension in the water are illuminated frontally, producing in the photograph a series of white points similar to snow flakes. It is therefore necessary to choose specialised equipment and the market today offers two different solutions. On one hand there are various amphibious cameras which are already watertight in themselves and do not need to be shut in a watertight case. The most famous is the Nikonos, a camera which has now reached its fifth model series and is equipped with automatic exposure and interchangeable (only out of the water!) lenses. Apart from the Nikonos there are other amphibious cameras which have a fixed optics installed which can, if so desired, be changed into a wide-angle lens with a special additional optics to place before the lens.

The other solution is to enclose a land camera in a special watertight case which allows access to the various commands so as to be able to use it in the same way as on land. Despite the fact that this seems an old-fashioned solution, it is still very valid and allows one to use a much wider series of lenses than the amphibious cameras. Naturally cameras suitable to close in these cases must be reflex monolens, which are the only ones which allow precise control over focusing and over the area really framed with the various lenses. Nowadays also one can make use of a series of really useful automatisms,

like the one for focusing and exposition, which help the photographer a great deal. Right from the first few metres down the use of an electronic strobe is indispensable, not so much to light up the scene which is often sufficiently lit up already by sunlight, but to revive the colours filtered by the stratum of water. These are in fact lost after the first few metres and pictures taken without artificial light even at only 10 metres depth will turn out to have a monochrome pale blue colour after development, entirely deprived of the vivid reds, pinks, oranges and yellows which make the underwater world so fascinating and varied. Underwater flashes are absurdly expensive and can even cost more than the camera itself. The required characteristics are soft, uniform and ample, though not necessarily strong, light, so as to sufficiently illuminate even the range embraced by a wide-angle lens. The power supply can be either dry batteries or rechargeable batteries, whilst for the exposition the models which work in automatism TTL in coupling with the camera are better; this automatism can, if necessary, be disconnected. As to films, only slides should be used. Negative films which provide colour prints give poor chromatic results because of the difficult and erroneous interpretation of the underwater colours by automatic printers. As far as sensitivity goes, films from 50-100 ISO are preferable to more sensitive films, in order to obtain a more defined and clear-cut image. Among the numerous accessories available on the market, extension tubes or additional lenses (in the case of amphibious cameras) are very useful, or a macro lens (with watertight case) in order to be able to photograph small organisms from near to, a type of photography which is not particularly difficult but which gives great satisfaction right from the start.

Motormarine amphibious camera made by the Japanese Sea and Sea (above) and a case in aluminium casting made by the Canadian Aqua Vision for the Nikon F90X, with a porthole for macro shots.

1,2,3 - **Grey Reef Shark** *(Carcharhinus amblyrhynchos)*

SHARKS

Open sea/reef - diurnal/nocturnal - solitary/gregarious - carnivorous - snorkelling/scuba - 0/70 m

The bad reputation that sharks bear was partly spread by the first experiences of diving, and always linked to hunting expeditions. Sharks are particularly attracted and excited by the vibrations of a wounded fish and therefore it is only natural that they should rush to the spot when a fish is harpooned and flounders bleeding in the water. Their entrance on the scene in these cases was typical of highly strung and excitable animals, determined to seize the bleeding prey, snatching it away from the divers. However, since underwater fishing has been prohibited in most tropical localities, the behaviour of sharks has totally changed: shy and suspicious, it is not easy to approach them and at the least sign of a diver following them they swim away, to the extent that it is difficult to take good photographs of them, unless one attracts them by offering food. Thus one should not feel worried when one sees a shark underwater and very soon one's feeling will be fascination for their infinite grace and their elegant and powerful way of swimming and behaving like lords of the sea. We must not, however, forget that they are predators endowed with powerful means of attacking which may leave unpleasant memories to imprudent or silly divers.

Sharks are cartilaginous fish and thus are related to rays, manta rays, eagle rays and electric rays.

One of the sharks which one is most likely to encounter on the coastal reefs is the Whitetip Reef Shark *(Triaenodon obesus)* which is elongated in shape and its dorsal and tail fins are tipped with white. It is often to be encountered resting on the sandy seabottom or inside caves where it may stay for a long time. It is active above all at night, when it hunts prey hiding in the gorges of the reef, by virtue of its elongated form which allows it to slip even into narrow gorges.

The Grey Reef Shark *(Carcharhinus amblyrhynchos)* is the leading actor in all the sea circuses or

4

5

6

7

8

16

9

4 - Whitetip Reef Shark *(Triaenodon obesus)*
5,7 - Leopard Shark *(Stegostoma fasciatum)*
6 - Scalloped Hammerhead Shark *(Sphyrna lewinii)*
8 - Silvertip Shark *(Carcharhinus albimarginatus)*
9,10 - Nurse Shark *(Nebrius ferrugineus)*

10

shark-feeding shows. Its body is decidedly stockier and it inspires a certain respect, reaching 175 cm in length. It can be recognised by a lighter strip on the dorsal fin, whilst the tail is edged with black.
Similar to the Grey Reef Shark, but with all its fins edged with white is the Silvertip Shark *(Carcharhinus albimarginatus)* which can grow to 180 cm and can be quite hostile, making forays at divers in order to drive them out of its territory.
An encounter with the Scalloped Hammerhead Shark *(Sphyrna lewinii)* is always exciting. Often they group together in shoals of a great number and can be recognised by the characteristic form of the head. They are considered potentially dangerous, but in reality have never bothered divers.
On the sea bottom one may come across the Leopard Shark *(Stegostoma fasciatum)* which derives its name from its beautiful spotted skin and which is completely innocuous. The Nurse Shark *(Nebrius ferrugineus)* is also harmless and likes to stay hidden inside the gorges of the reef during the day.

17

Dasyatididae (Stingrays) - Myliobatidae (Eagle rays) - Mobulidae (Manta rays) - Torpedinidae (Electric rays)

Stingrays, like sharks, are cartilaginous fish, and their body has adapted for life on the sea bottom. Stingrays have a terrible defense weapon at their disposal, a serrated and poisonous spine positioned on their tail, which if necessary can inflict extremely painful wounds. They are often to be met with on the sandy seabottom partially covered with sediment or in caves. They feed on molluscs, crustaceans and little fishes which they manage to hunt out even if they are totally hidden in the sand thanks to a sophisticated reception system that allows them to perceive the weak electric field produced by a living organism. The most widespread species in the Maldives is the Black Stingray *(Taeniura melanospilos)* which can grow to a diameter of a metre and a half.

Eagle rays *(Aetobatis narinari)* are, on the other hand more frequently encountered whilst they swim in mid-water, rhythmically moving their

12

13

11 - Black Stingray *(Taeniura melanospilos)*
12 - Detail of the eye of a Black Stingray
13 - The dangerous spine of a Black Stingray
14 - Manta ray *(Manta sp.)*

14

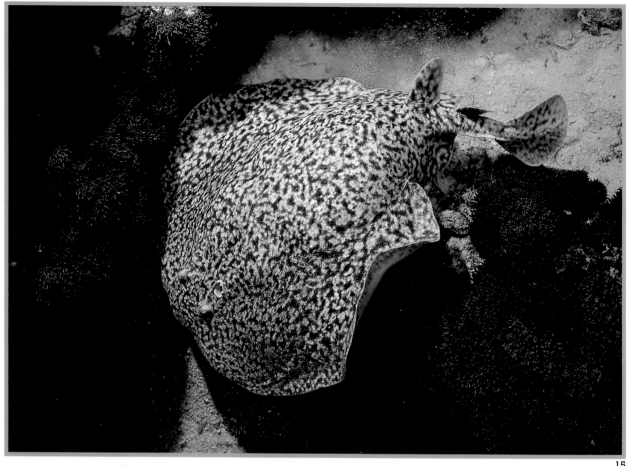

15 - Electric ray *(Torpedo sinuspersici)*
16 - Spotted eagle ray *(Aetobatis narinari)*

great "wings". They have a pointed face which gives them a strange appearance and are distinguished by their beautiful marbled skin and their whip-like tail which is about three times the length of their body. Like the stingrays, eagle rays also have venomous spines (from 1 to 5), positioned, however, at the base of the tail.

The large manta rays *(Manta birostris)* were once believed to be dangerous but are actually completely harmless, feeding exclusively on plankton which they capture by swimming with their enormous mouth wide open. On the sides of their head they have two cephalic fins which are used to channel the water towards their mouth. Manta rays can grow to an enormous size, up to 5-6 metres. They tend to swim around near certain banks, where an encounter with them is not unlikely.

Electric rays look like stingrays, but they have a roundish body and a shorter tail without spines. They have a sophisticated electrical system to stun their prey, composed of organs rather similar to batteries which can emit an electrical discharge of considerable intensity.

Sphyraenoidea - Barracuda

Open sea - diurnal/nocturnal - solitary/gregarious -
carnivorous - snorkelling/scuba - 0/50 m

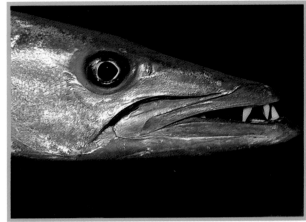

It is natural to feel rather afraid when face to face
with a large barracuda seeing its terrible teeth and
cold searching look, typical of predators, so close
to us. Its behaviour towards divers is, however, only dictated by curiosity, which when satisfied, the
barracuda will very calmly swim away moving its
powerful tail almost imperceptibly. Barracudas often group together in shoals of hundreds and
these sometimes form a kind of circle round divers
which is a magnificent sight.

The "giant" of the group is the *Sphyraena barracuda*, a fish which can reach over 2 metres in length
and 40 kg in weight. This fish is held to be the sole
member of the family responsible for attacks on
man, all of which took place in turbid waters where
the movements of a swimmer could be mistaken
for the vibrations of a wounded fish.

17

17 - Great Barracuda *(Sphyraena barracuda)*
18,19 - Shoals of barracudas *(Sphyraena sp.)*

18   19

Carangidae - Trevally

Open sea - diurnal - solitary/gregarious - carnivorous - snorkelling/scuba - 0/60 m

One of the most exciting encounters is that with the silver trevallies, open sea dwellers that arrive in the shallow waters as if by magic and are always in perpetual motion. They are tireless swimmers with a perfect hydrodynamic form who often group together in large shoals when young, becoming solitary when they are adult. Some species reach a considerable size, being able to grow to over a metre and a half in length. They are very strong predators with very few enemies in the underwater world and they patrol the external edge of the reef, ready to drop down like hawks on weak or heedless prey. The most common species are the Bluefin Trevally *(Caranx melampygus)* and the Bigeye Trevally *(Caranx sexfasciatus)*.

20 - Trevally *(Caranx lugubris)*
21 - Bigeye Trevally *(Caranx sexfasciatus)*
22 - Bluefin Trevally *(Caranx melampygus)*

20

21

22

Ephippidae - Platax or batfish

Open sea - diurnal - solitary/gregarious - carnivorous - snorkelling/scuba - 0/25 m

The platax are among the most elegant creatures of the reef, especially in youth when the dorsal and ventral fins are fully developed, the appearance of which earned them their name of batfish. Their body is very compressed laterally, and in the adult is round with the skin covered with shiny silver scales which are broken up by darker vertical stripes. Their shape is little suited to swimming and in fact platax cannot boast of speed and prefer to remain still in mid-water in compact little groups, swimming to the bottom every now and again to capture invertebrates and other small prey on which they feed. In the Maldives, two species may be encountered: *Platax orbicularis* and *Platax teira*. The first can be distinguished by its more prominent face whilst the second has an almost vertical profile.

23 - Circular Batfish *(Platax orbicularis)*
24 - Detail of the head of a juvenile batfish
25 - Longfin Batfish *(Platax teira)*

23

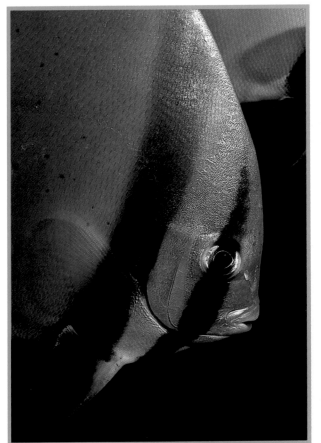

24

25

26

27

Lutianidae - Snappers

Open sea/reef - solitary/gregarious - diurnal/nocturnal - carnivorous - snorkelling/scuba - 5/150 m

Several large and powerful fish belong to this family, for example, the Twinspot Snapper *(Lutjanus bohar)* which can reach a metre in length and is one of the great predators of the reef, always ready to rush to the scene at the least sign of commotion. It may be encountered in the shallows, but it prefers deeper waters where it lives, solitary and wary. Other representatives of the same family, for example the Bluestripe Snappers *(Lutjanus kasmira)*, with their bright yellow colouring, group together in dense shoals which sometimes form real living walls. The *Lutjanus monostigma*, which like to hide in caves, also gather together in groups, though their groups are smaller than the preceding. As do the *Lutjanus gibbus* which prefer waters which are not too deep and are rich in currents where they collect and remain during the daytime.

26 - Twinspot Snapper *(Lutjanus bohar)*
27,30 - Bluestripe Snapper *(Lutjanus kasmira)*
28 - *Macolor macularis*
29 - *Aphareus furca*
31 - Two-spot Banded Snapper *(Lutjanus biguttatus)*
32 - *Lutjanus monostigma*
33 - Humpback Red Snapper *(Lutjanus gibbus)*

28

29

30

31

32

33

34

35

Lethrinidae

Open sea/reef - solitary/gregarious - diurnal/nocturnal - carnivorous -snorkelling/scuba - 5/120 m

Lethrinidae are often confused with Lutianidae which they resemble in shape and feeding habits, a mistake which also derives from the fact that both families are called "Schnapper" in German. They are strong predators that feed on other fish, molluscs and crustaceans. Some species, for example the *Lethrinus erythracanthus*, can grow to 70 cm in length; they are solitary and prefer to stay in caves and shady crevices. The Large-eyed Sea Bream *(Monotaxis grandoculis)* derives its name from its large round eyes; its juvenile colouring is characterised by the presence of four vertical black bands, alternating with light bands, which disappear in the adult. *Gnathodentex aureolineatus* is typically gregarious and it can be found in groups several scores strong. *Lethrinus xanthochilus* is not common and it does not usually let divers approach it; it includes holothurians in its diet, prey which is spurned by most fish.

34 - Emperor *(Lethrinus erythracanthus)*
35 - Large-eyed Sea Bream *(Monotaxis grandoculis)*
36 - Gold-striped Bream *(Gnathodentex aureolineatus)*

36

Caesionidae - Fusiliers

Pelagic - diurnal - gregarious - carnivorous - snorkelling/scuba - 5/60 m

Fusiliers form large shoals which sometimes envelop the diver in dense clouds of fish, rather as anchovies do in the Mediterranean. They are diurnal fish which feed on little animal organisms near the reef. They will be encountered mainly on the external reef edge where they create a gay motif with their gradation of colour tones which range from red to electric blue, from pale blue to yellow according to the species. To escape from predators, rather than take refuge in the gorges of the reef as many other reef inhabitants do, they prefer to trust in their swimming ability.

37

38

37 - *Pterocaesio trilineata*
38 - Dark-banded Fusilier
      (*Pterocaesio tile*)
39 - *Pterocaesio tile*
      and *Pterocaesio pisang*
40 - Yellowfin Fusilier
      (*Caesio xanthonota*)

39

40

Echeneidae - Remora

Pelagic - diurnal - solitary/gregarious - carnivorous - snorkelling/scuba - 0/100 m

Remoras are well known for their habit of getting themselves carried around by large marine animals such as sharks, manta rays, turtles, Napoleonfish, whales and dolphins to which they attach themselves with a sucker they have on their heads. This sucker is derived from the metamorphosis of a dorsal fin and allows the remora to attach itself to the host with considerable tenacity, picking up the leftovers of their banquets. In exchange they offer a toilette service, freeing their hosts from the parasites which afflict most of the large marine animals. Remoras do not always live in symbiosis with other fish and they may be encountered alone or in large groups which sometimes remain stationary under anchored boats. They can even reach a metre in length.

41,42 - Remoras *(Echeneis naucrates)*

41

42

Muraenidae - Morays

Reef - diurnal/nocturnal - solitary - carnivorous - snorkelling/scuba - 2/50 m

The snake-like form and smooth scaleless skin of the morays allows them to slip with great ease into the most narrow crevices of the reef, where they remain holed up during the daytime and where, mostly by night, they hunt their prey. Right from ancient times morays have had a bad reputation, accused of devouring rebel slaves thrown as food to them by the ancient Romans. In actual fact they are not at all dangerous if not provoked or wounded and are actually rather timid, often hiding themselves away in their den when a diver is approaching. Their exceptional strength, large size and powerful set of teeth must warn one, however, against silly familiarity which could result in serious wounds. The Giant Moray *(Gymnothorax javanicus)* can reach a frightening size of over 2.5 metres in length. Morays undergo a sex change during growth, changing from male to female.

43

43 - Giant Moray *(Gymnothorax javanicus)*
44 - *Gymnothorax favagineus*

44

45,46 - Giant Moray
   (*Gymnothorax javanicus*)
47 - *Gymnothorax favagineus*

46

47

48

Serranidae

Two important groups of fish belong to this family; the Anthias and the Groupers.

Anthias

Reef - diurnal - gregarious - carnivorous - snorkelling/scuba - 0/15 m

These fish are a few centimetres long and are extremely brightly coloured, brightening up the shallow waters of the reef, where they live in dense shoals, with red, orange and purple brush strokes. They feed on little planktonic organisms during the daytime and spend the night hidden in cracks and small holes, well protected from predators. The males have a brighter appearance and colouring than the females and have harems of ten or so "concubines" for every male. On the death or disappearance of the male, one of the adult females of the same group takes its place, changing sex and colouring.

Among the most common species in the Maldivian waters, the Scalefin Anthias *(Pseudanthias squamipinnis)* and the beautiful Yellow tail Anthias *(Pseudanthias evansi)* which is half yellow and half purple, must be mentioned.

48 - Yellow tail Anthias *(Pseudanthias evansi)*
49,51 - Scalefin Anthias (male) *(Pseudanthias squamipinnis)*
50 - Scalefin Anthias *(Pseudanthias squamipinnis)*
52 - Anthias *(Pseudanthias ignitus)*

49

50

51

52

53

54

53,54 - Coral Grouper
        (*Cephalopholis miniata*)
55,56 - Black-saddled Coral Trout
        (*Plectropomus laevis*)
57 - Peacock Rock Cod
        (*Cephalopholis argo*)

Groupers

Reef - diurnal/nocturnal - solitary - carnivorous -
snorkelling/scuba - 5/200 m

Groupers are among the strongest predators of the
reef and each has its own territory which it bravely
defends from the raids of other groupers. Its very
form is typical of a marauder, with a strong body
and the lower jaw more prominent than the upper,
often with its terrible teeth partially visible. Their
habitat stretches from the first few metres of the
reef to the sea bed at well over 100 metres. They
particularly like caves and wrecks, where they
hide if frightened. They can be very brightly
coloured as in the case of the Coral Grouper
(Cephalopholis miniata) which is a brilliant red
colour with pale blue spots or the Lunartail
Grouper (Variola louti) which can be distinguished
by its sickle-shaped tail. The Greasy Grouper (Epinephelus tauvina) is, on the other hand, very
mimetic and it remains so motionless in the
crevices of the reef that sometimes it is difficult to
see it. The Black-saddled Coral Trout (Plectropo-
mus laevis) is of a decidedly conspicuous size,
able to grow longer than a metre and weigh more
than 10 kg. Its juvenile colouring is exactly the op-
posite of what it will be as an adult: as a juvenile it
is white with vertical black bands and a yellow tail,
whilst as an adult it becomes dark with lighter vertical bands and a dense series of pale blue markings.

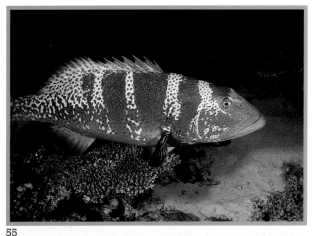

55

56

57

58 - Slender Grouper
  (Anyperodon leucogrammicus)
59 - Four-saddle Grouper
  (Epinephelus spilotoceps)
60 - *Epinephelus polyphekadion*
61 - *Cephalopholis polleni*
62 - Greasy Grouper
  (Epinephelus tauvina)
63 - White-spotted Grouper
  *(Epinephelus
  caeruleopunctatus)*

58

61

59

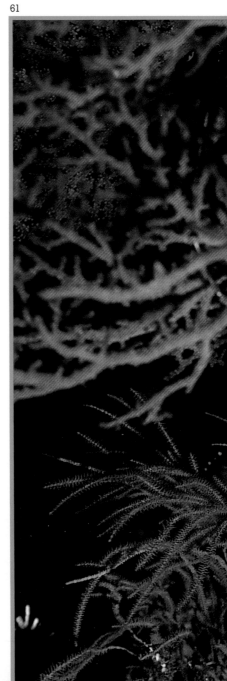

60

62

63

64 - Redmouth Grouper
  (*Aethaloperca rogaa*)
65 - Blacktip Grouper
  (*Epinephelus fasciatus*)

64

65

Haemulidae - Grunts or sweetlips

Reef - diurnal/nocturnal - gregarious - carnivorous - snorkelling/scuba - 2/40 m

Grunts like to gather together in little groups and it is not rare to come across these groups of 5-10 fish in shallow water, motionless, sheltered by the large coral formations. The most common species in the Maldives is the Oriental Sweetlips *(Plectorhynchus orientalis)* which has a striking "pyjama" coat with a series of black and white horizontal stripes, whilst head, fins and tail are yellow with black markings. The juvenile livery is very different, mottled yellow and brown, and much more mimetic. The Silver Grunt *(Diagramma pictum)* which is of a silvery-grey colour, may be met with in deep caves and can even reach 90 cm in length. The name "Grunt" comes from the ability of this group of fish to produce sounds by gnashing their teeth and amplifying the sound with their swimbladder. They are carnivores and feed mainly on molluscs and crustaceans.

66

67

66,70 - Oriental Sweetlips
(*Plectorhynchus orientalis*)
67 - Oriental Sweetlips
(juvenile colouring)
(*Plectorhynchus orientalis*
68 - Many-spotted Sweetlips
(*Plectorhynchus chaetodonoides*)
69 - Silver Grunt
(*Diagramma pictum*)

68

69

70

Labridae - Wrasses

Reef - diurnal - solitary - carnivorous -
snorkelling/scuba - 0/50 m

Not only is the family of wrasses among the largest in number of species, but almost all representatives of this family vary in colouring according to age, displaying often entirely different colouring as juveniles, in the intermediate stage and as adults. Thus it is not always easy to identify the various species, although their way of swimming is characteristic of the family and soon recognizable. Wrasses use their pectoral fins to swim, which makes them swim with a swaying motion. The giant of the family is the well-known Napoleonfish *(Cheilinus undulatus)* which can reach a size of over 2 metres long and nearly 200 kg in weight. This fish derives its name from the strange protuberance on its head, similar in shape to the head-

gear of the Emperor Napoleon. Other species, on the other hand, are very small, for example, the Cleaner Wrasse *(Labroides dimidiatus)* which attends to the toilette of other fish, principally predators, freeing them from parasites. The colouring of the wrasses is among the most striking of the reef dwellers and often one is enraptured by such beauty and chromatic variety. They are exclusively diurnal fish which spend the night well protected in the cragginess of the reef, where they take on less bright and more mimetic colours.

71 - *Halichoeres leucoxanthus* (Male)
72 - Diana's Hogfish *(Bodianus diana)*

71

72

41

73

74

75

76

73 - Slingjaw Wrasse, female *(Epibulus insidiator)*
74 - Slingjaw Wrasse, male *(Epibulus insidiator)*
75 - *Cheilinus hexataenia*
76 - Bandcheek Wrasse *(Cheilinus digrammus)*
77 - Axilspot Hogfish, female or juvenile
      (Bodianus axillaris)
78 - Speckled Wrasse *(Anampses meleagrides)*

77

78

79

80

81

82

83

84

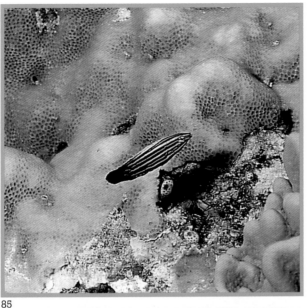

85

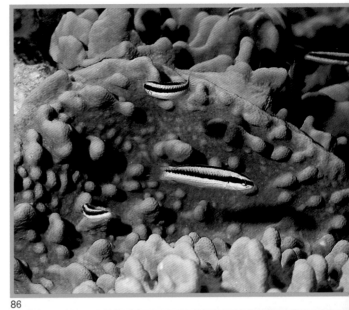

86

87

88

79 - Checkerboard Wrasse *(Halichoeres hortulanus)*
80 - Juvenile colour phase of Clown Coris *(Coris aygula)*
81 - *Macropharyngodon bipartitus* (Male)
82 - *Macropharyngodon bipartitus* (Female)
83 - *Halichoeres vrolikii* (Male)
84 - *Halichoeres cosmetus* (Male)
85 - *Labropsis xanthonota* (Female or juvenile)
86 - *Thalassoma amplycephalum*
87 - Six-barred Wrasse *(Thalassoma harwicke)*
88 - *Thalassoma quinquevittatum*
89 - Moon Wrasse *(Thalassoma lunare)*

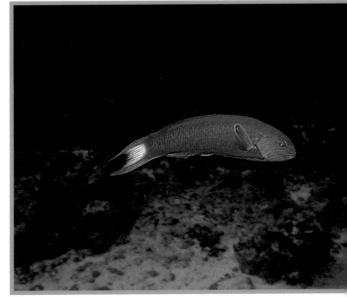

89

90 - Thick-lipped Wrasse
    (*Hemigymnus fasciatus*)
91 - Napoleonfish
    (*Cheilinus undulatus*)
92 - *Labroides bicolor*
93 - Cleaner Wrasse
    (*Labroides dimidiatus*)
94 - Redbreasted Wrasse
    (*Cheilinus fasciatus*)

92

93

94

47

95

Pomacanthidae - Angelfish

Reef - diurnal - solitary - omnivorous - snorkelling/scuba - 0/50 m

The name angelfish may derive from the beautiful colouring of these fish or from their rather developed fins which vaguely look like wings.

Almost all the species have a juvenile colouring which is so different from the adult colouring that it is difficult to believe that it is the same fish.

All representatives of this family have a strong spine on the branchial preoperculum, which provides an easy way to tell them apart from the Butterflyfish *(Chaetodontidae)* which look very like them.

Their sex changes with age: female when young and male thereafter. The latter defend a rather large territory where 2 to 5 females live. If the male disappears, the largest and most dominant female changes sex and takes his place.

Their diet includes a wide variety of organisms, both plant and animal according to the species. Some angelfish, especially in their youth, may occasionally change into cleaner fish freeing other fish from irritating parasites.

95 - **Emperor Angelfish (juvenile)** *(Pomacanthus imperator)*
96 - **Emperor Angelfish** *(Pomacanthus imperator)*
97 - **Semicircle Angelfish** *(Pomacanthus semicirculatus)*
98 - **Royal Angelfish** *(Pygoplites diacanthus)*

96

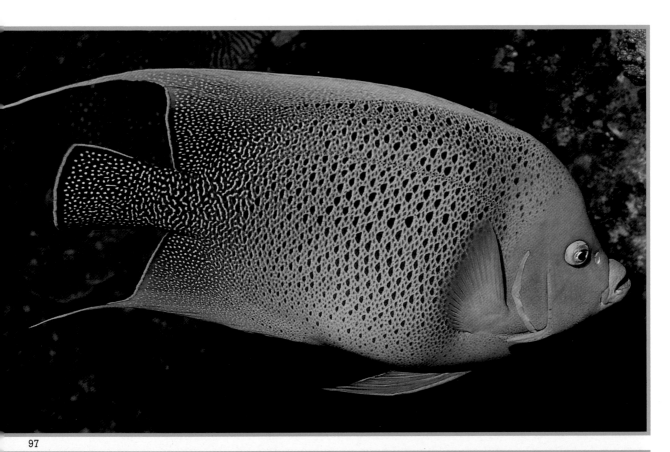

97

98

99

100

99 - Three-spot Angelfish *(Apolemichtys trimaculatus)*
100,101 - Blue-faced Angelfish
        (Pomacanthus xanthometopon)

102 - Klein's Butterflyfish *(Chaetodon kleinii)*
103 - Meyer's Butterflyfish *(Chaetodon meyeri)*
104 - *Chaetodon xanthocephalus*

101

Chaetodontidae - Butterflyfish

Reef - diurnal - gregarious/solitary -
carnivorous/omnivorous - snorkelling/scuba - 0/40 m

102

Butterflyfish derive their name from their beautiful bright colours, their roundish shape and their slow and rather "fluttering" way of swimming which makes them look just like butterflies. They have a narrow, flattened body, suitable for slipping with ease into even the most intricate coral structures, where they seek refuge when a predator approaches. Their face is tapering and thin, suited to feeding on coral polyps or other small organisms hidden in the chinks of the reef. Two species, *Forcipiger flavissimus* and *F. longirostris* have a very long and very thin face suited to attacking prey hidden even in the narrowest fissures. Butterflyfish are rarely to be sighted alone, they always form fixed couples which remain together for the rest of their lives. Members of the genus *Heniochus*, on the other hand, assemble in groups of as many as a hundred which look like huge flocks of birds. At night butterflyfish sleep well protected in the crevices of the reef, trying to escape the nocturnal hunting of the morays and other predators. When they swim during the day, their colouring contributes to their defensive strategy; it is broken up by bands, streaks and "false eyes" which serve to deceive and confuse the ideas of their enemies.

103

104

105

106

107

108

109

105 - *Chaetodon citrinellus*
106 - Triangular Butterflyfish *(Chaetodon triangulum)*
107 - Chevron Butterflyfish *(Chaetodon trifascialis)*
108 - Double-saddled Butterflyfish *(Chaetodon falcula)*
109 - Red-fin Butterflyfish *(Chaetodon trifasciatus)*

110

110 - Long-nosed Butterflyfish
   (Forcipiger longirostris)
111 - Bennett's Butterflyfish
   (Chaetodon bennetti)

111

112

113

114

115

112 - Teardrop Butterflyfish *(Chaetodon unimaculatus)*
113 - *Chaetodon oxycephalus*
114 - Racoon Butterflyfish *(Chaetodon lunula)*
115 - Black-backed Butterflyfish *(Chaetodon melannotus)*
116 - Madagascar Butterflyfish
     (Chaetodon madagascariensis)

116

117 - *Scarus rubroviolaceus* (Female)
118 - *Scarus rubroviolaceus* (Male)
119 - Bicolour Parrotfish *(Cetoscarus bicolor)*

Scaridae - Parrotfish

Reef - diurnal - herbivorous - solitary/gregarious -
snorkelling/scuba - 0/20 m

If one holds one's breath under water, it is not unlikely that one may hear the characteristic noise
produced by parrotfish when they scrape corals
with their powerful beak, feeding on the thin layer
of algae that covers them. Only the vegetal part is
digested, whilst the calcareous bits are powdered
and turned into fine white coral sand, which is expelled in the form of pleasing little clouds. The
production is so abundant that parrotfish are rightly held to be one of the principal producers of the
lovely sand which tourists like so much.

These fish are characteristically diurnal and swim
alone or in small groups. During the night they
hide in the crevices of the reef where they stand
out in torchlight because of their brilliant colouring. Some species secrete a kind of cloud of mucus in the night, in which they wrap themselves as
in a cocoon, preventing nocturnal predators from
noticing their smell and finding them out.

Parrotfish have very different colouring in the various periods of their lives, radically changing
colour with their sex change from female first to
male afterwards.

117

118

119

120

121

122

120 - Singapore Parrotfish
    (Scarus prasiognathos) (Male)
121 - Tricolour Parrotfish
    (Scarus tricolor) (Male)
122 - *Scarus frenatus* (Male)
123 - Dorsal fin of parrotfish
    (Scarus sp.)

123

124

125

Acanthuridae - Surgeonfish

Reef - diurnal - gregarious/solitary -
herbivorous/omnivorous - snorkelling/scuba - 0/50 m

Compressed air cylinders are not necessary in order to see these fish, which are some of the principal inhabitants of the coastal waters and can be seen by any snorkeller in a few spans of water, sometimes grouped together in shoals of several dozen fish. Their name derives from the mobile spines and bone plaquettes, sharp as scalpel blades, which are located on either side of the caudal peduncle and accentuated with a mark of a contrasting colour. These blades are used both for defense against predators, and for fighting with members of the same species. Divers should avoid touching them, a thing which is easy to do in the night time, when the fish sleep in the cracks in the reef. The wounds inflicted by a struggling fish can be deep and painful. Some species, such as *Naso vlamingii* and *Naso hexacanthus*, can change colour in an incredible fashion, passing from their usual dark colouring to a very light bluish shade, which they usually take on when they let the cleaner fish clean them. Among the stranger species the Spotted Unicornfish *(Naso brevirostris)* must be mentioned, which in spite of its Latin name, has a very long protuberance like a beak on its face.

126

127

128

129

130

124 - *Acanthurus xanthopterus*
125 - Sleek Unicornfish, light colouring
    (*Naso hexacanthus*)
126,128 - Blue Surgeonfish (*Acanthurus leucosternon*)
127 - Sailfin Surgeonfish (*Zebrasoma desjardinii*)
129 -Vlaming's Unicornfish (normal colouring)
    (*Naso vlamingii*)
130 - Blue-lined Surgeonfish (*Acanthurus lineatus*)
131 - Spotted Unicornfish (*Naso brevirostris*)

131

132

Balistidae - Triggerfish

Reef - diurnal - solitary - herbivorous/omnivorous - snorkelling/scuba - 3/50 m

On the external edge of the reef one often meets shoals of little pale blue fish with an extremely forked tail, which slip into narrow cracks when the diver approaches, leaving only their tail sticking out. These are Redtooth Triggerfish *(Odonus niger)* which are equipped, like all triggerfish, with a strange trigger mechanism which blocks one of the rays of the dorsal fin in an erect position, so that however much their tail is pulled in an attempt to extract them from the hole, they are stuck fast and will not come out. Triggerfish have strong teeth which allow them to break up the shells of the shellfish and sea urchins on which they feed. The most photogenic triggerfish in the Maldives is the Clown Triggerfish *(Balistoides conspicillum)*, which is an amazing black with large white marks. The giant of the family is the Titan Triggerfish *(Balistoides viridescens)* which becomes aggressive during the reproduction period, attacking without hesitation whosoever approaches the large circular nest where the male guards the eggs.

132 - Titan Triggerfish *(Balistoides viridescens)*
133 - Half-moon Triggerfish *(Sufflamen chrysopterus)*
134 - Blue Triggerfish *(Pseudobalistes fuscus)*
135 - Boomerang Triggerfish *(Sufflamen bursa)*
136 - Redtooth Triggerfish *(Odonus niger)*
137 - Clown Triggerfish *(Balistoides conspicillum)*
138 - Orange-striped Triggerfish *(Balistapus undulatus)*

133

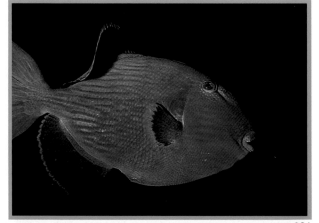

134

135

136

137

138

139

Monacanthidae - Filefish

Reef - diurnal - solitary/gregarious - omnivorous - snorkelling/scuba - 2/40 m

Filefish are related to triggerfish and are easily distinguished by an extremely developed ray in the first dorsal fin, which can be blocked, like the triggerfish, in an upright position by a trigger mechanism. *Aluterus scriptus*, which has beautiful colouring decorated with pale blue, can grow to a metre in length; it is a circumtropical fish, but not common in the Maldives and has a very varied diet which includes hydrozoa, sea anemones, gorgonians, tunicates and algae. The little Harlequin filefish *(Oxymonacanthus longirostris)*, on the other hand, live in pairs or in little groups in among the coral, the polyps of which they feed on. *Paraluteres prionurus* looks exactly like the little pufferfish *Canthigaster valentini* which has a powerful poison which keeps predators away. The "disguise" works and the little filefish in this way manages to protect itself well.

140

139 - Harlequin Filefish *(Oxymonacanthus longirostris)*
140 - *Paraluteres prionurus*
141 - Scribbled Leatherjacket *(Aluterus scriptus)*

141

Pomacentridae - Damselfish and clownfish

Reef - diurnal - solitary/gregarious - herbivorous/omnivorous - snorkelling/scuba - 0/25 m

Pomacentridae are one of the species which most enliven the tropical shallows, literally enveloping the coral formations in dense clouds of fish, like a crowded city in the rush hour. Damselfish belong to this family, and are quite like the Mediterranean damselfish, but with colouring that in certain species, like the Blue-green chromis *(Chromis viridis)* takes on a delicate pale blue-greenish hue. Other species, like the Sergeantfish *(Abudefduf sp.)* have their colouring broken by a series of vertical bands and are larger. The most well known representatives of the family are undoubtedly the famous clownfish, maybe the most photographed of all tropical fish, partly because of their bright colours but principally due to their habit of living in among the stinging tentacles of sea anemones (see box).

The diet of the *Pomacentridae* is very varied: some feed on plankton, others are omnivorous and eat everything: algae, small invertebrates and zoo-plankton. The solitary and territorial species are very brave, ready to defend their territory valiantly even when faced with intruders who are much larger than them.

142

143

142 - Clark's Anemonefish *(Amphiprion clarkii)*
143 - Twobar Humbug *(Dascyllus carneus)*
144 - Black-footed Clownfish *(Amphiprion nigripes)*

144

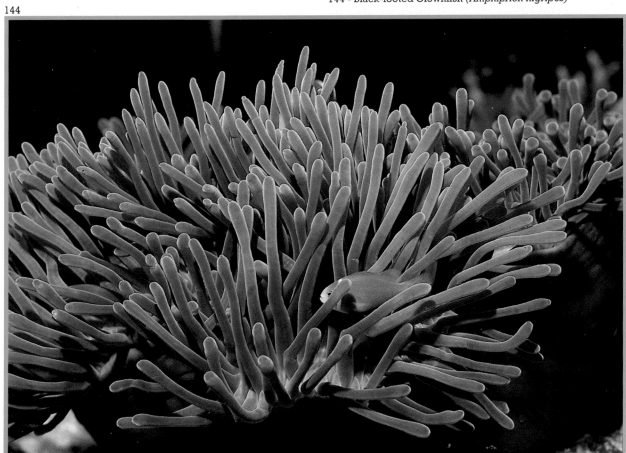

145

146

147

148

149

CLOWNFISH

The name derives from the brightness of their colouring, with bands of a dazzling white, which calls to mind the ceruse used by clowns to colour their cheeks. They live exclusively in close contact with stinging sea anemones which other fish can not go near without being paralyzed and killed by the potent poison. The clownfish are, however, protected by a thick mucus which allows them to swim about, happy and safe in the midst of the stinging tentacles, making rapid sorties every now and again to catch the small zooplankton organisms on which they feed. In exchange for this protection, the fish are perfect tenants, keeping their host perfectly clean by freeing it from all organic remains or sediment. This is a typical case of mutualistic symbiosis, that is, when two organisms exchange reciprocal favours. Clownfish have a very pleasant face and are very brave, especially when the female lays her eggs at the base of the sea anemone. The males in this case do not hesitate even to attack divers, with rapid spurts and harmless little bites. A large sea anemone is usually host to a "family" made up of a couple of adult fish and other smaller ones. The biggest and most dominant fish is the female. If it disappears, the largest male adult changes sex and takes its place while another male, the next biggest, reaches sexual maturity fast and takes on reproductive functions.

150

145 - Golden Chromis
(*Chromis ternatensis*)
146 - Narrowbar Damsel
(*Plectroglyphidodon dickii*)
147 - Humbug Damselfish
(*Dascyllus aruanus*)
148 - Domino, juvenile
(*Dascyllus trimaculatus*)
149 - Blue-green Chromis
(*Chromis viridis*)
150 - Half-and-half Chromis
(*Chromis dimidiata*)
151, 152, 154 - Black-footed
Clownfish (*Amphiprion nigripes*)
153 - Jewel Damselfish
(*Plectroglyphidodon lacrimatus*)

151

152

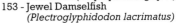

153

154

155

156

Mullidae - Mullets or goatfish

Reef - diurnal - gregarious - carnivorous - snorkelling/scuba - 0/20 m

Mullets are hard workers, continually intent on rooting about on the sea bed, their head buried in the sand and a thick cloud of dust which signals their passage. They are easily recognizable because of their two long barbels located under the jaw. These contain chemical sense organs and are used to search for food. The males also use them during courtship, shaking them showily.

Mullets are all carnivorous and feed mainly on small invertebrates which hide in the sand, but they do not spurn the odd little fish. When they are intent on finding food it is quite easy to approach them, less so, on the other hand, when they are resting motionless on the sea bed. At night they lie asleep on the sand, taking on, as many other fish do, less noticeable colouring

155 - Goatfish *(Parupeneus barberinus)*
156 - *Parupeneus pleurostigma*
157,160 - Yellowfin Goatfish *(Mulloides vanicolensis)*
158 - Doublebar Goatfish *(Parupeneus bifasciatus)*
159 - Yellowsaddle Goatfish *(Parupeneus cyclostomus)*

157

158

159

67

161

162

163

164

165

161 - *Amblyeleotris aurora*
162 - *Amblygobius hectori*
163 - Magnus Goby *(Amblyeleotris steinitzi)*
164 - Maiden Goby *(Valenciennea puellaris)*
165 - *Istigobius decoratus*
166 - *Fusigobius sp.*

166

Gobiidae - Gobies

Reef - diurnal - solitary/gregarious - carnivorous - snorkelling/scuba - 2/30 m

This is the most numerous family of fish, numbering over 800 species worldwide.
They do not have a very striking appearance and often are actually transparent and difficult to see. They usually stay on the sea bed where they dig burrows in which they take refuge at the least sign of danger. Some gobies live in symbiosis with shrimps from the *Alpheidae* family, sharing the same refuge. It is a mutualistic symbiosis: the shrimps dig the hole and keep it clean with unceasing "bulldozer" work, whilst the gobiidae stand guard over it at the entrance, as the shrimps can see very little, being almost blind. To transmit information they constantly touch the body of the gobies with their antennae and it transmits an "all clear" or "look out, danger in sight" signal.

70

Microdesmidae - Dartfish

Reef - diurnal gregarious - carnivorous - scuba - 5/50 m

These fish are a few centimetres long and are characterised by symmetrical dorsal and ventral fins, which makes them look like little darts. The genus *Nemateleotris* has a very long erect ray on its dorsal fin, which gives these little fish a magnificent appearance and, together with their wonderful colours, makes them photographic favourites. They live in couples and take refuge, darting fast as lightening into their hole dug in the sand, when danger approaches. More elongated in shape and of a larger size is the *Ptereleotris evides* which as a juvenile forms little groups, whereas as an adult it lives strictly in couples. All dartfish feed on the small animal organisms which make up zooplanckton.

167

167 - *Nemateleotris decora*
168 - Dartfish *(Ptereleotris evides)*
169 - Fire Goby *(Nemateleotris magnifica)*

168

169

170

Blenniidae - Blennies

Reef - diurnal - solitary - herbivorous/carnivorous - snorkelling/scuba - 2/30 m

These are small fish of an elongated form with a long and continuous dorsal fin which live in the shallow waters of the reef and along the external reef edge. Despite their seemingly peaceable appearance, they are rather aggressive animals, ready to defend their territory bravely even against much larger animals. They can often be seen inside holes in the coral, from which their agreeable little head pokes out. Some are masters in the art of imitation. The false cleaner fish *(Aspidontus taeniatus)*, for example, looks very like the Cleaner Wrasse and even imitates its way of swimming, thus gaining the trust of other fish who need a toilette and then at the crucial point tearing off a piece of the unfortunate "client's" skin. The representatives of the genus *Plagiotremus*, which have very similar appearance to that of other *Blenniidae* or to the young Cleaner Wrasse are also able "tricksters".

171

170 - **Striped Blenny** *(Ecsenius lineatus)*
171 - *Plagiotremus phenax*
172 - *Plagiotremus rhinorhynchos*
173 - *Meiacanthus smithi*
174 - *Plagiotremus sp.*

172

174

173

Scorpaenidae - Scorpionfish

Benthonic - solitary - diurnal/nocturnal - carnivorous -
snorkelling/scuba - 2/30 m

These are sedentary fish which are sadly famous for their poisonousness. They are all voracious predators who swallow their prey whole, opening their large mouth out of all proportion and making sudden darts. Some are very lovely, like the lionfish *(Pterois)* which look like feathered butterflies and probably use their striking appearance to remind potential predators that they are poisonous. Others, on the other hand, like the large *Scorpaenopsis diabolus*, *S. oxycephala* and the terrible stonefish, use their incredible mimetism to ambush their prey. They merge so totally with the surrounding environment that they are often unidentifiable even on a careful and close examination of the reef. They prevalently live in shallow waters and thus are a considerable danger for bathers, who may stand on them and be pricked by the poisonous spines. The pain is excruciating, accompanied by swelling, breathing difficulties and in some cases even death. The most poisonous of all is the stonefish *(Synanceia verrucosa)* and it is also the most mimetic, looking entirely like the sea bed around it.

175

175 - Clearfin Lionfish *(Pterois radiata)*
176 - Tassled Scorpionfish *(Scorpaenopsis oxycephala)*

176

177

178

179

180

177 - *Taenionotus triacanthus*
178,181 - Scorpionfish *(Pterois miles)*
179,182 - Ragged-finned Lionfish *(Pterois antennata)*
180 - Stonefish *(Synanceia verrucosa)*

74

181

182

183

184

Antennaridae - Frogfish

Reef - nocturnal - solitary - carnivorous - snorkelling/scuba - 0/30 m

These fish look like scorpionfish, but are actually completely harmless for man, not having spines connected to poison glands. Masters in the art of camouflage, frogfish become virtually invisible on whatever type of sea bed they find themselves. Not only is their spherical and rather amorphous body difficult to identify, but one's amazement increases on noticing how they use their pectoral fins to ''walk'' on the sea bed. The first ray of the dorsal fin is metamorphosed into a kind of fishing rod with lure, which is moved to attract the prey, whilst the ''fishers'' lie completely motionless. The trick often works, exciting the curiosity of a fish, which draws near and inexorably ends up in the huge jaws of the frogfish, the which are able to swallow prey even longer than themselves. Encounters with frogfish are not frequent, above all due to the difficulty in managing to identify them when they lie motionless on the reef.

183,184,185,186 - Frogfish *(Antennarius sp.)*

185

187

Synodontidae - Lizardfish

Benthonic - diurnal - solitary - carnivorous - snorkelling/scuba - 3/20 m

The long narrow body and the head adorned with a large mouth vaguely call to mind the shape of a lizard, whence the name. They live lying on the sandy sea bed and on the reef, completely immobile, making use of the extreme mimetism of their colouring. Sometimes they bury themselves in the sand leaving only their eyes poking out and making identification even harder. When prey approaches, they dart at it very fast and seize it with their long sharp teeth. Members of the same species are included among the prey on which they feed, an act of cannibalism which is also common in many other predatory species.

188

189

187 - Common Lizardfish *(Synodus variegatus)*
188 - Lizardfish *(Saurida gracilis)*
189 - *Synodus sp.*

Syngnathidae - Pipefish

Reef - diurnal - solitary - carnivorous - snorkelling/scuba - 0/30 m

The name comes from the extremely tapering and slender shape of the body which ends at the front in a long tube-shaped face, making these fish look like little snakes. The body is armoured by a series of bony rings and its total length is not usually over 15-20 cm. Pipefish feed on minute crustaceans which are swallowed by sucking in water through the trunk-like snout. The eggs laid by the female are incubated by the male in a special ventral pouch.

190

190,191,192 - Gilded Pipefish *(Corythoichthys schultzi)*

191

192

193

195

196

197

194

Holocentridae - Squirrelfish and soldierfish

Reef - nocturnal - carnivorous - scuba - 10/50 m

When one looks into caves opening on the external slope of the reef, one almost always comes across attractive red fish, which stand out pleasingly in the dimness. These are squirrelfish which are of a characteristic very bright reddish-orange colour and have large eyes which testify to their nocturnal habits. They pass the hours of daylight in places protected from the light waiting for the night which they pass in looking for crustaceans, which are their favourite food. The largest member of the family is the Sabre Squirrelfish *(Sargocentron spiniferum)* which can grow to 45 cm and has a bony spine on its preoperculum. It lives alone or in small groups of 5-10 fish in the craggy depths of the reef and shows no fear of divers, but fixes its large round eyes on them full of curiosity. Soldierfish *(Myripristis sp.)* are, on the other hand, smaller in size and form dense shoals in the darker recesses of the caves.

193 - Spotfin Squirrelfish *(Neoniphon sammara)*
194,198 - Sabre Squirrelfish *(Sargocentron spiniferum)*
195 - *Neoniphon opercularis*
196 - Violet Soldierfish *(Myripristis violacea)*
197 - Soldierfish *(Myripristis adusta)*
199 - Blotcheye Soldierfish *(Myripristis murdjan)*
200 - *Myripristis vittata*
201 - Squirrelfish *(Sargocentron caudimaculatum)*
202 - *Sargocentron diadema*

198

199

201

202

203

204

205

Priacanthidae - Bigeyes

Reef - nocturnal - carnivorous - scuba -
10/50 m

These fish are very like the *Holocentridae* in appearance, colouring and nocturnal habits, but belong all the same to a different family. Sometimes they leave the holes where they live during the day and assemble in large groups, which can be made up of several dozen individuals. They feed mostly on planktonic forms, like crustacean and fish larva. They possess a considerable ability to alter their colouring: in a few seconds they can change from a very bright red to a greyish-silver hue, with vaguely pale reddish tones. *Priacanthidae* are widespread throughout the Indian and the Pacific Oceans and recently examples of Bullseye *(Priacanthus hamrur)* have been found off the Tunisian coasts, indicating probable migration through the Suez Canal.

203,204,205 - Bullseye *(Priacanthus hamrur)*
206 - Largetooth Cardinalfish
    (Cheilodipterus macrodon)
207 - Wolf Cardinal *(Cheilodipterus artus)*
208 - *Cheilodipterus quinquelineatus*

Apogonidae - Cardinalfish

Reef - nocturnal - solitary/gregarious - carnivorous - snorkelling/scuba - 5/50 m

206

The shape of cardinalfish is unmistakable: a large head, two separate dorsal fins, big round eyes and a mouth which is out of proportion with the size of the fish. They are nocturnal fish par excellence, which during the day take refuge in cracks, caves or ravines in the reef away from sunlight. At night they hunt predominantly little crustaceans or zooplankton. Some species have a formidable set of teeth, for example the Largetooth Cardinalfish (*Cheilodipterus macrodon*), whose teeth protruding from its jaw give it a rather aggressive appearance. Many cardinalfish are solitary, others swim in couples or in small groups, but there are some small and semi-transparent species which form spectacular and enormous shoals at the top of the corals.

It is the male cardinalfish who has the role of protecting the eggs and there is no safer or more efficient system than that adopted: the eggs are gathered together in his large mouth and kept there until they hatch, the males obviously giving up eating for this period. One sometimes sees one of these fish with its mouth so full of eggs as to have to keep it slightly open.

207

208

209

Cirrhitidae - Hawkfish

Reef - diurnal - solitary - carnivorous - snorkelling/scuba - 2/40 m

These are one the easiest photographic subjects as they are completely immobile and thus allow ample time for the photographer to approach and then frame and focus. This is a small family of fish which pass their time resting on the reef waiting for a small fish or crustacean, their favourite food, to pass within their range. The Horseshoe Hawkfish *(Paracirrhites arcatus)* and the Blackside Hawkfish *(P. forsteri)* stay on the corals, whereas the Longnose Hawkfish *(Oxycirrhites typus)* prefers the fans of the gorgonians where it is well camouflaged by the red squares which cover its body. The phenomenon of sex change also takes place in this group: first female and then, if necessary, male. The males are very territorial and have a little private harem of females.

209, 213 - Horseshoe Hawkfish *(Paracirrhites arcatus)*
210 - Longnose Hawkfish *(Oxycirrhites typus)*
211 - Pixy Hawkfish *(Cyrrhitichtys oxycephalus)*
212 - Blackside Hawkfish *(Paracirrhites forsteri)*

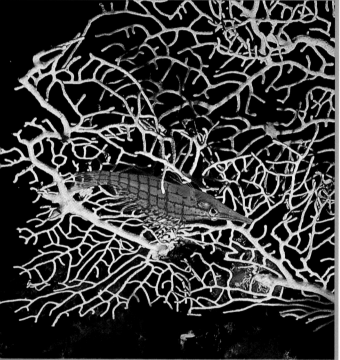

210

211

212

213

Ostracidae - Trunkfish

Reef - diurnal - solitary - omnivorous - snorkelling/scuba
- 5/25 m

In trunkfish the scales are metamorphosed into bony plates of a hexagonal or polygonal shape, joined to one another so as to form a strong shell, from which fins and tail stick out. This shape certainly does not favour swimming and trunkfish move slowly, generally only using the anal and dorsal fins and resorting to the caudal fin only in case of rapid flight. The pectoral fins are used, on the other hand, for moving sideways and allow acrobatics and about-faces worthy of a helicopter. They eat a large quantity of algae, sponges, worms, molluscs and sea urchins, which they manage to grind up with their strong teeth, after having turned them over with powerful water blowing. Some species can give off a poisonous mucus when the fish is under stress. The poison (ostracitoxin) destroys red blood cells and can be lethal for other fish, but it can also be lethal for the trunkfish itself if it is in a narrow space with little water.

214

214, 215 - Cube Trunkfish (juvenile) *(Ostracion cubicus)*

215

216

217

218

216,217,219 - Cube Trunkfish (adult)
(Ostracion cubicus)
218 - Whitespotted Boxfish (Ostracion meleagris)

219

Tetraodontidae - Pufferfish

Reef - diurnal - solitary - omnivorous - snorkelling/scuba - 5/25 m

In normal conditions pufferfish have an elongated shape but, if threatened, they can suck in water very fast to fill a diverticulum situated in the ventral area of the stomach, considerably increasing in this way the size of their body and taking on their characteristic spherical shape. This operation is, however, stressful for the fish and one should never make them "puff up" just for the fun of it or in order to take a photograph. *Tetraodontidae* produce a very powerful poison which is present in their blood and in certain organs, which if eaten can be lethal even for man. Precisely because of this high risk they are a culinary challenge and are cooked in the Orient following an elaborate recipe, the famous Fugu, which causes a certain number of deaths every year.

220

221

220 - Scribbled Pufferfish *(Arothron mappa)*
221 - Whitespotted Pufferfish *(Arothron meleagris)*
222 - Sharpnose Pufferfish *(Canthigaster valentini)*

222

223

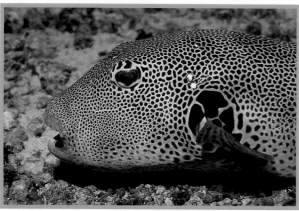

224

223,226 - *Canthigaster tyleri*
224 - Starry Pufferfish (*Arothron stellatus*)
225 - *Canthigaster bennetti*

225

226

Diodontidae - Porcupinefish

Reef - nocturnal - solitary - carnivorous -
snorkelling/scuba - 5/25 m

Porcupinefish can swell up like pufferfish by sucking in large quantities of water. However they also
possess another very effective weapon: the surface of their body is covered with sharp spines
which are normally flattened, but which stand up
perpendicularly when the fish swells up. Very few
predators dare to attack such a well protected fish,
though some sharks do not seem to mind and porcupinefish are regularly found, for example, in the
stomachs of tiger sharks. Teeth which are fused together in robust dental plates allow these fish to
grind up the shells of shellfish and crustaceans
and even to tackle sea urchins, which are habitual
prey for them. Most of this species is nocturnal and
passes the day hidden in caves and ravines.

227 - Bleeker's Porcupinefish *(Diodon liturosus)*
228 - Porcupinefish *(Diodon hystrix)*

227

228

229

230

PORIFERA - SPONGES

It is difficult for the novice to imagine sponges different in form and consistency from those commonly used to wash with. In actual fact these are only a limited section of the huge number of species that live in the sea (around 10,000) which sometimes only appear as little encrustant layers, or in the shape of a candelabra, cup-shaped, trunk-shaped or as formless heaps. It is not easy to classify them under water given that identification is very often made by examining the calcium carbonate or siliceous spicules which make up the skeleton under a microscope. The sponges illustrated here can easily be seen in the Maldives and are all *Demospongiae*, that is sponges with siliceous spicules embedded in a spongy structure called "spongin". To feed, sponges make water flow inside their structure through little pores, retaining the tiny food particles.

231

232

229 - *Xestospongia exigua*
230 - Orange Sponge
231 - Sponge
232 - *Leucetta chagosensis*
233 - Sponge *(Poeciloscleridae)*

233

234

CNIDARIA OR COELENTERATES

To this *phylum* belong all the numerous animals which are constituted by polyps, that is of little animals shaped like a calyx attached to a base, with a ring of stinging tentacles and a mouth which opens in the middle of them. Polyps can be single, as with the sea anemones, or can form large colonies. They can also be jellyfish form, floating freely in the water and often the two forms alternate: a fixed polyp produces a jellyfish asexually, the which, in turn, produces a polyp sexually.

234 - Slab Fire-coral *(Millepora platyphylla)*
235,236 - White Stinging Sea-fan *(Lytocarpus philippinus)*
237 - Stylasterid Coral *(Distichopora violacea)*
238 - *Distichopora sp.*
239 - Net Fire-coral *(Millepora dichotoma)*

235

236

Hydrozoa

Hydrozoa are very widespread in the Maldives, above all the hard forms known as "fire-coral" which divide the role of important reef constructors with the coral. The two main species are *Millepora dichotoma*, which has an arborescent appearance and is of a browny-yellowish colour with white tips, and *Millepora platyphylla* which forms undulating vertically-growing structures with a whitish upper edge. Both of these species are often confused with corals although they are hydrozoa and are armed with powerful stinging cells which cause painful "burns" if they touch the skin. Another species which can be found in crevices and fissures, especially where wave movement is violent, or at greater depths, particularly round the northernmost islands, is the very beautiful *Distichopora* which forms little colonies of an intense bluish-purple or pinky-orange, also with white tips. Plumed sea-fans look completely different, like small flexible feather-shaped plants and they also have a powerful sting. The best known species in the Maldives is the White Stinging Seafan *(Lytocarpus philippinus)*.

237

238

239

Scyphozoa (Jellyfish)

Jellyfish are not popular with divers and bathers because of the painful burns that can result from touching their tentacles. Only some species are, however, stinging for man and they are all very beautiful fragile animals equipped with a very sophisticated system for catching their food. Jellyfish usually drift with the current being unable to swim against it effectively with the rhythmic contractions of their umbrella, which do however produce a slight movement. Like little fishing boats, some jellyfish trail long thin filaments armed with stinging cells (nematocysts) which on the slightest contact inject a powerful paralyzing poison. Using this system they catch little planktonic organisms and tiny fish which swim near the water surface. One of the most common in the Maldives is the Moon Jellyfish *(Aurelia aurita)*, which is completely harmless for man. It has a flattened discoid structure and sometimes groups together in large and very spectacular shoals.

The Upsidedown Jellyfish *(Cassiopea andromeda)* is very unusual: it lies with its umbrella on the sea bottom and its tentacles pointing upwards. It can easily be distinguished on the sandy sea bottom in shallow water where it is a tasty titbit for turtles.

240

240 - Upsidedown Jellyfish *(Cassiopea andromeda)*
241 - Moon Jellyfish *(Aurelia aurita)*

241

242

Anthozoa - *Octocorallia*

The members of this class have eight tentacles and are always colonial.

GORGONIANS

Gorgonians construct arborescent, tuft-shaped and fan-shaped structures which sometimes reach a considerable size. They grow perpendicular to the current, so that the little polyps can catch the largest possible quantity of plankton.

Precisely because of this characteristic one sees gorgonians positioned almost barring certain caves or passages in which the current flows, whilst on the exposed slopes of the reef they almost always place themselves vertically, like huge hands stretched out towards the open sea. Due to their tree-like appearance and bright colours they are one of the great attractions for divers. Their skeleton, apart from a few exceptions, is entirely horny and is characterised by a certain elasticity and flexibility.

The huge Giant Gorgonian Sea-fan *(Subergorgia mollis)* reaches the largest size, up to over 2 metres span, and it grows where the current is fairly strong, providing in its turn support for crinoidea and some bivalvia.

Junceella, a filiform gorgonian which grows at great depths, generally attached to hard substrates or on the sandy bottom of caves, is very unusual in its whip-like form. The end of the whip is slightly bent and the colour, if lit up by a spotlight, is bright red.

243

242 - Gorgonian Sea-fan
243 - Gorgonian Sea-fan
244 - Gorgonian Sea-fan *(Melithaea sp.)*

244

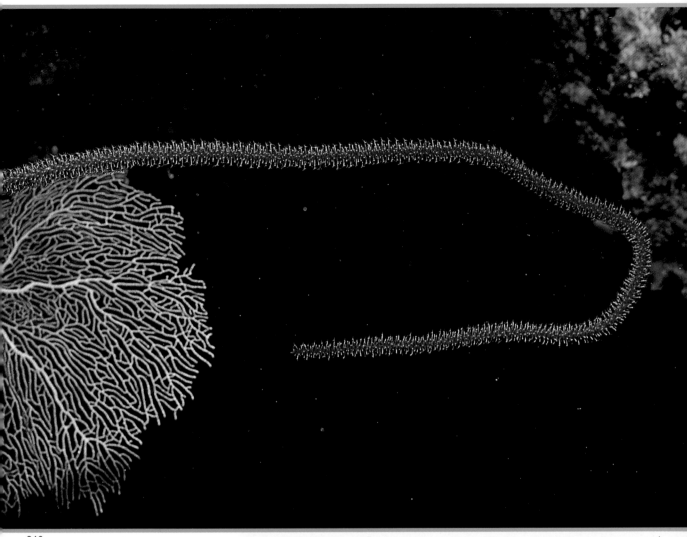

246

245, 247, 248 - Giant Gorgonian Sea-fan
    (Subergorgia mollis)
246 - Whip Coral *(Junceella rubra)*
249 - Gorgonian sea-fan
250 - Gorgonian sea-fans
251 - Gorgonian sea-fan *(Euplexaura sp.)*
252 - Gorgonian sea-fan *(Melithaea sp.)*

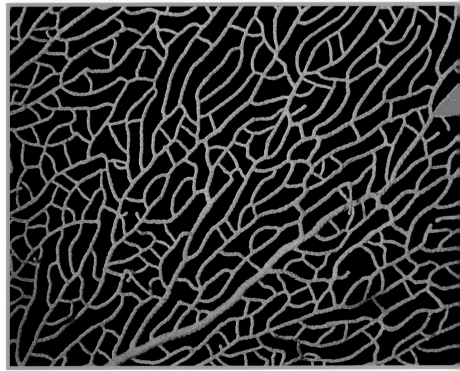

247

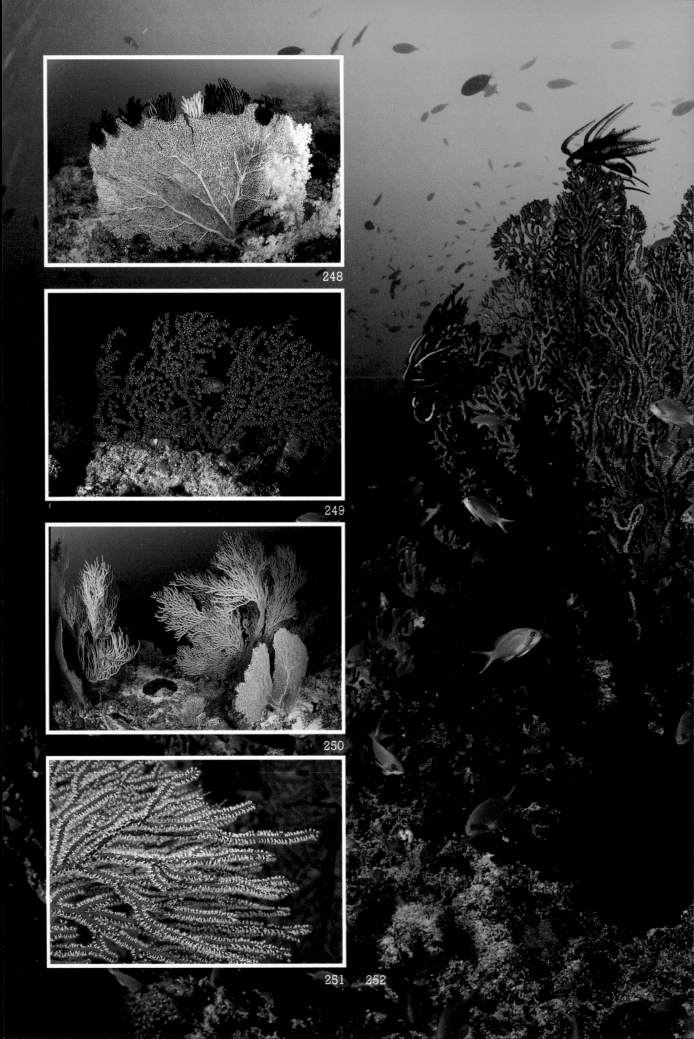

248

249

250

251   252

ALCYONACEA OR SOFT CORALS

Soft corals have a right to a place among the organisms which thrill one most when diving in a tropical sea, and in some areas they vie with corals in abundance, covering large stretches of reef. As their name suggests they have no rigid structure and the polyps are supported by a fleshy mass in which there are sometimes calcareous spicules. The various families look so different that it is difficult to believe that they are closely related: one passes from slender forms like flowers to animals of a rubbery appearance and a uniformly grey colour. The polyps have eight tentacles *(Octocorallia)*, they feed on plankton brought to them by the current and are more or less retractable into the fleshy mass which makes up the structure of the colony.

The most loved, admired and photographed are the various species of *Dendronephtya* and *Scleronephtya*, usually known as alcyonacea. These have a tree-like structure of translucent matter, in which the calcareous spicules can be seen quite well. Colour ranges from pink to dark red, from yellow to light blue, from orange to violet. In some diving zones entire vaults of grottoes are festooned with *Alcyonacea* which tend to take on monochrome hues: yellow, blue, pink.

Similar in appearance, but not translucent and of a uniform yellowish-white, is the *Lithophyton arboreum*, a species which is very common in the waters of the Maldives.

Sarcophyton looks like a sponge of a greyish-green colour which appears whitish when the polyps are expanded with their corollas of tentacles extended.

253

254

255

256

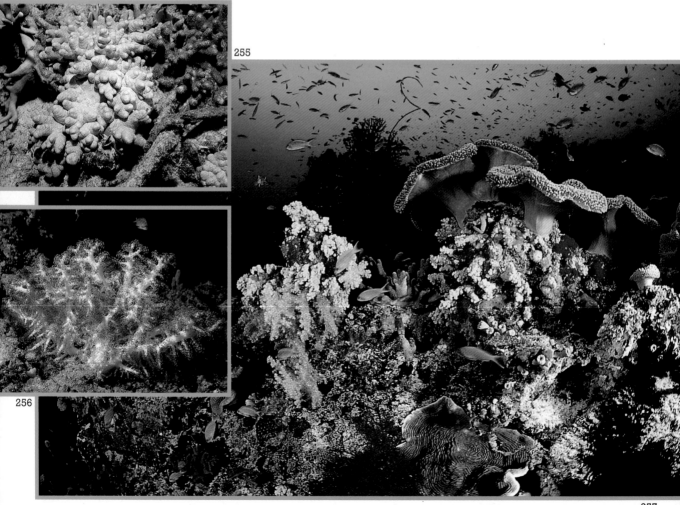

257

258

259

260

261

253, 254, 257, 260 - *Sarcophyton sp.*
255 - *Sinularia sp.*
256 - Soft coral
258 - Soft coral
259, 261 - Alcyonacea *(Dendronephtya sp.)*
262 - Alcyonacea *(Scleronephtya corymbosa)*

262

Anthozoa - *Hexacorallia*

The organisms belonging to this class are characterised by the presence of polyps whose tentacles either number six or a multiple of six. There are both solitary and colonial forms.

STONY CORALS

Madrepores or stony corals are the main builders of the coral reefs and are mostly colonial animals. It is easy to identify them as belonging to the *Hexacorallia* by counting their tentacles, which must number six or a multiple of six. Every polyp is able to secrete calcium carbonate which enlarges and strengthens the structure of the colony. The polyps feed on zooplankton and zooxanthellae, algae which live in symbiosis with the corals, and are largely responsible for the colours that these may assume. Their shape and size are incredibly varied, being able to form very branchy tree-like structures, towers and monoliths, large spherical heaps like rocks, intricate serpentine labyrinths, broad umbrella or canopy roofs and many other forms. Corals offer a refuge to most of the coralline fauna, which find certain protection from predators between the branched and rigid structures.

The acropores are among the most widespread and abundant species in all tropical seas and are often used by juvenile fish as a nursery because their very branched shape does not allow larger predators to follow the little prey into the structure. They often have gradatory colouring which shades off to pink and violet tones, derived from zooxanthella.

Grandiose structures which are heavy and hard like real rocks belong to the *Porites* genus. These often house polychaetes and bivalves inside them. *Seriatopora* has slender forms, which make a kind of bush with pointed tips to the "branches".

The *Favus* genus takes its name from its honeycomb structure.

Differing from the other corals which are almost always colonial, those belonging to the *Fungia* genus are made up of a single polyp, except some species which are, however, only made up of a few

263

264

265

266

polyps. Their name is derived from the likeness of their numerous septa to the lamellas of fungae.

Fungia and *Herpolitha*, the first of a discoid form, the second elongate, are often taken for dead corals by novices, because during the day they show no movement whatsoever and the tentacles are not visible. At night, however, the polyp's tentacles come out from the interstices between the lamellas and it feeds on plankton.

The corals of the *Dendrophyllia* genus are to be seen on the vaults of grottos and ceilings of shady covered places. During the day they often draw their corona of tentacles into the polyp, making them look like little hard tubes. At night they expand their tentacles transforming their appearance to look like little bunches of yellow or orange flowers.

Beautiful arborescent colonies of *Tubastrea* are also to be found at a certain depth. In some areas there is a high concentration of them, forming real "petrified forests". They are very fragile and if bumped, literally fall to pieces. At night the polyps expand their tentacles, making the colony look like the branch of a tree in flower.

263 - Staghorn Coral *(Acropora sp.)*
264 - *Diploastrea sp.*
265 - *Cynarina sp.*
266 - Spiny Row Coral *(Seriatopora sp.)*
267 - Extended tentacles of *Goniopora sp.*
268 - *Fungia sp.*
269 - *Dendrophyllia sp.*

267

268

269

270, 271, 272 - *Tubastrea sp.*
273 - *Fungia sp.*

270

271

272

273

274

ANTIPATARI - BLACK CORAL

Black coral in the strict sense of the term belongs to this order, a material which right from ancient times was gathered, worked and sold as jewelry. The most typical forms are very different from one another. The genus *Antipathes* has an arborescent form and can easily grow to a metre and a half in height. Its tips are very slender and flexible whilst it becomes robust and tough near the base. This is the black coral which is worked into bracelets and other trinkets and which takes on a shiny black colour once it is smoothed and polished. Although it is on sale in the villages, its commerce officially banned in the Maldives and should not be encouraged. The other form, of the *Cirrhipathes* genus, is whip-like and might be confused with the whip gorgonians of the *Junceella* genus, except that its polyps have six tentacles rather than eight like the polyps of the latter.

274, 275 - *Cirrhipathes sp.*

275

ACTINIARIA - SEA ANEMONES

The structure of sea anemones is like a cylinder attached to the substrate with its base and they have no skeleton. They have a large number of tentacles furnished with strong stinging cells which they use to catch the little organisms, such as fish and crustaceans, on which they feed. The prey is paralyzed by the poison and then brought into the mouth which opens in the centre of the tentacles, and digested. When disturbed, sea anemones quickly contract their body, retracting mouth and tentacles. They are almost always host to a couple or an entire family of clownfish which are immune to their poison thanks to the protective mucus which covers their body. In return, the clownfish keep the sea anemone clean and sometimes induce other prey to venture in among their tentacles. The lower part of some sea anemones can be a very bright colour which varies from pink to scarlet, but which can also take on purplish hues.

276

277

276 - *Radianthus ritteri*
277 - Sea anemone
278 - *Gyrostoma helianthus*

278

109

279

280

ANELLIDA (WORMS) - Polychaeta

This class numbers several thousand species which are subdivided into two main categories: mobile forms and forms which live attached to the substrate. The first have a vermiform appearance and are often equipped with a series of tufts of stinging bristles which cause intense pain on contact with the skin. These worms are strong predators with robust jaws which actively hunt their prey, wriggling through the meanders of the reef.

The sedentary forms have an entirely different appearance, looking like little flowers or tufts of feathers. They live inside a thin tube which they themselves secrete and which is fixed to the substrate or, in some cases, completely buried in the calcium carbonate of the huge brain corals, as in the case of *Spirobranchus giganteus* which can assume the most varied colours. They feed by filtering water through their showy branchial tufts, retaining the plankton. If disturbed they withdraw instantaneously into their tube.

279 - **Christmas Tree Worm** *(Spirobranchus giganteus)*
280 - **Fan Worm** *(Sabellastarte sanctijosephi)*
281 - **Terebellid Worm**

281

CRUSTACEA

Their body is protected by a strong protective shell which, being rigid, does not grow; as the animal develops it must, therefore, shed its old shell like a cast-off garment. When this happens, the new shell has already formed under the old, but it is still soft and thus this is a very delicate period in the life of a crustacean which is at the mercy of predators until the carapace hardens. Most crustaceans have separate sexes and fertilization is mostly internal. Particularly important are shrimps,

which very often clean fish (see box). Several species of lobster live in the Maldives, well hidden in the gorges of the reef during the day, but easy to sight at night, patrolling the shallow waters of the reef. The Spiny Lobster *(Panulirus versicolor)* is one of the largest, recognizable by its bright colouring: green and white stripes with pink and pale blue details. Hermit crabs have soft and undefended abdomens and have to find an abandoned shell in which to establish their home; it then needs to be changed during their growth as their size increases. The Spotted Hermit Crab *(Dardanus tinctor)* often carries a few sea anemones on its shell, making use of their stinging power to avoid being preyed on. Real crabs have their abdomen protected by their rigid shell and furthermore can boast of an effective deterrent: a good pair of claws which if necessary they know how to use with great ability.

282

282 - *Dardanus megistos*
283 - *Galathea sp.*

283

284

285

284 - Hermit crab *(Dardanus sp.)*
285 - Spiny Lobster *(Panulirus versicolor)*
286 - Coral Crab *(Carpilius convexus)*

CLEANER SHRIMP

*S*ometimes one notices large fish like groupers and moray eels waiting on the threshold of a hole with their mouths wide open. This is not an attitude to frighten their enemies, but rather a delicate moment in their toilette. They are, in fact, at a "cleaning station", run by shrimps of various species, the most common of which belong to the species **Stenopus hispidus**. They work industriously to free the large predators from the parasites which live on their skin, in their mouth and in their gills. The only way to get rid of these troublesome parasites is to depend on the treatment of the cleaner fish or these small crustaceans, which slowly inspect their client's body, removing the parasites on which they feed, with their claws. The shrimps of the **Stenopus** genus seem to use their long white antennae to "stroke" their guests before the cleaning treatment in order to restrain their aggressiveness, an indispensable condition before entering the mouth of a fish which could easily swallow them. It is not hard to distinguish these shrimps at night, when their cleaning work ceases, hiding away in the fissures of the reef where they live in very stable couples which stay together all their life.

286

MOLLUSCS

In the world of shells nature achieves a degree of beauty and inventiveness in shape and colour which is rarely to be found in other creatures. The porcelain-like sheen of many gastropods, the brightness of their colours and the patterns which decorate the surface, make them such beautiful jewels that right from ancient times they have been cult and collection objects on the part of all peoples and were often used as currency in commercial exchanges. It must not be forgotten, however, that shells are nothing else but the "house" of living beings and that every time a shell is picked up and brought to the surface, an animal is killed in a cruel way. Collection of shells is rightly forbidden everywhere in the Maldives and care is also necessary with shells which seem to be without an animal; these are often inhabited by hermit crabs which are not visible because they are hiding in the spirals further inside the shell. Prominent among the various classes are that of the gastropods, provided with a single shell which is often spiral-shaped, or without a shell (nudibranchs), and that of the bivalves, with a shell made up of two valves.

Gastropods - *Prosobranchia (Shells)*

Prosobranchs are usually of a classic spiral-form, with the shell more or less elongated, although there are striking exceptions with roundish shapes like eggs, or elongated like spindles or bristling with sharp points and protuberances, which appear to have very little in common with the classic spiral-form.

There are both herbivorous and carnivorous prosobranchs; the latter use a sophisticated organ called a radula to make a hole in the shells of other shellfish on which they feed. Cowries must be enumerated among the most beautiful gastropods; their marvellous shiny ovoidal shells are possibly those most coveted by collectors worldwide.

Cone-shells are also very beautiful, but they should not be touched because of a very effective defensive-offensive system, which allows some species to let fly a dart which is connected to a poison gland at their prey or at a predator. These darts are so poisonous in some species (*Conus textile* and *C. geographus*) that they cause the death of the shell collector.

287 - *Conus arenatus*
288 - *Turbo petholatus*
289 - *Conus geographus*
290 - Auger Shell *(Terebra maculata)*

287

288

289

290

291

292

Gastropods -
Opisthobranchia (Nudibranchs)

As their name suggests, these molluscs are "nude", that is, without a shell, and they are reminiscent of slugs in appearance and in their way of crawling around. In most of the species their colours are very bright and showy because as they have no shell they have to resort to special defense strategies so as not to be preyed on. Some species feed on hydrozoa and are able to transfer a part of their stinging cells into their own tissues, so as to become stinging themselves. Others cover their bodies with the calcareous or siliceous spicules of the sponges on which they feed, managing to construct a sufficiently rigid and unappetising shell as to be spurned by predators. Still other species possess special glands which secrete repellent substances. Their brilliant colours make them one of the favourite subjects of underwater photographers, who manage to photograph them without too much difficulty thanks to the slowness of their movements.

291 - *Phyllidia sp.*
292 - *Phyllidia bourguini*
293 - *Chromodoris sp.*

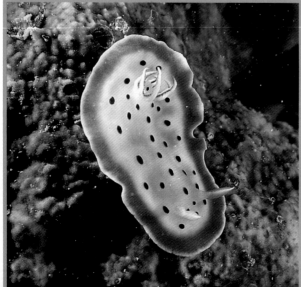

293

Bivalves

In this case the shell is made up of two valves which fit together perfectly, joined by a hinge made up of an elastic ligament, which is often assisted by teeth which also have a hinge function. Powerful adductor muscles close the shell which stops many predators from eating the delicious mollusc, but these muscles give way to the very strong traction of the arms of some starfish or the tentacles of octopuses. Sometimes the shell itself is broken up by the strong teeth of certain fish, like triggerfish and rays. They are among the most prolific egg producers of all marine animals: some species release several million in the water, but only a small section of these manage to pass the larval stage and the first few months until they have a shell which is sufficiently hard to withstand predators. Bivalves live near the sea bed, buried in the sand, inserted in the reef or fixed to gorgonians. Most species feed by filtering water by means of a two-siphon system: the "inhalent" one draws in the water, the "exhalent" expels it after the gills have retained the plankton.

294

295

294 - **Wing-oyster** (*Pteria sp.*)
295 - **True Oyster** (*Lopha cristagalli*)
296 - **Thorny Oyster** (*Spondylus aurantius*)

296

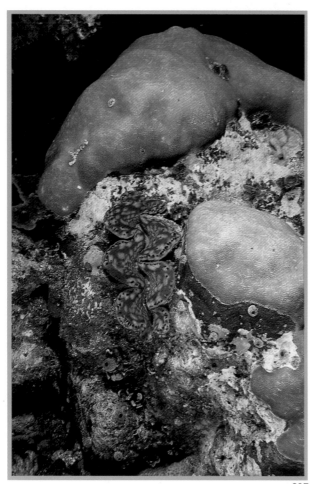

297

TRIDACNIDAE GIANT CLAMS

*W*hoever swims in shallow coastal waters where there are coral formations is struck by the very bright colouring and unusual shape of the tridacnidae or giant clams. These bivalves have turned themselves over, positioning themselves with the hinge which unites the two shells downwards and the opening between them upwards. Furthermore, just like a dress a few sizes too big, the mantle of the animal, with an elegant frill on its edge, spills luxuriantly out of the shell. The colouring of the mantle is extremely varied and showy, ranging from electric blue to green, from yellow to brown. This colouring is derived from microscopic algae (zooxantellae) which are "cultivated" by the mollusc, which then feeds on a part of them. The clam adopts its unusual position precisely in order to expose its body to sunlight, so that the growth of zooxantellae is as abundant as possible. The name "killer clam" comes from the size of the **Tridacna gigas** of the Indian and Pacific Oceans: it can grow to over a metre long and 250 kg in weight and has stimulated a wealth of tales because of the extraordinary strength of its adductor muscles which, according to the legends, have drowned pearl fishers who carelessly put a foot into the open valves which closed on them and held them down.

297, 298 - Giant Clam *(Tridacna maxima)*

298

ECHINODERMS

To this *phylum* belong organisms which are so different from one another that it is difficult to believe that they are in some way related. A common characteristic is five-rayed symmetry which is clearly visible in starfish and brittle stars and rather less so in sea urchins, feather stars and sea cucumbers. Another distinguishing characteristic is the presence of calcareous plates under the skin, which in some cases form real shells, as in the case of the sea urchins. Echinoderms usually have separate sexes, though some species are hermaphrodite.

Crinoidea (Feather stars)

For divers feather stars are some of the most loved and photographed organisms because of their fragile and pretty shape, like a cluster of feathers, and their beautiful colours. Given that they feed on plankton carried by the current, they usually climb up the gorgonians stretched out towards the open sea, so as to have access to a greater food supply. Sometimes they assemble in groups which look like gaily coloured bunches of flowers. They do not like the light and therefore pass the day in the fissures of the reef, waiting for the dark when finally they can leave their refuge and creep up to the highest places which are most exposed to the current. At greater depths where only faint light arrives, it is possible to see them during the day as well, moving their brightly coloured arms lazily. Feather stars have a little central body from which their feathered arms, which are very fragile but easily regenerated, protrude. On the lower part of their body there are short cirri (special clinging feet), with which they walk and cling to the substrate.

299 - *Himerometra sp.*
300 - *Comanthus sp.*
301 - Feather stars *(Crinoidea)*

299

300

301

Ophiuroidea (Brittle stars)

Brittle stars look like slender starfish, with a very small discoid body from which protrude their slender and extremely mobile arms which have earned them the name of "serpentine stars". These arms are smooth in some families, whilst in others they have numerous sharp spines which look like little bristles, but are actually rigid and can easily penetrate the skin even through protective gloves. Once they enter the skin, these spines break and cause great pain, therefore one should take care where one puts one hands, especially when swimming through gorgonians growing at the entrance to grottoes and crevices at a certain depth. Brittle stars are prevalently nocturnal and pass the daylight hours hidden in cracks and narrow fissures in the reef. The spiny ones, well protected by their terrible spines, often stay out, clinging to the gorgonians or sponges where they can easily be seen.

302

303

302, 303 - *Ophiotrix sp.*
304 - Slate-pencil Urchin *(Heterocentrotus mammillatus)*
305 - Diadem Urchin *(Diadema setosum)*

304

Echinoidea (Sea urchins)

Reef sea urchins have a roundish-shaped body, bristling with spines, which are both a defense weapon and used to jam themselves in the reef to avoid being preyed upon by triggerfish and other fish which manage to break up their strong shell. Some species, on the other hand, which live buried in the sand have a flat body covered with short spines. The mouth, surrounded by five strong teeth, opens on the bottom of the animal so that it is easy for it to crop algae and the detrius on which it feeds. The most widespread in the Maldives is the Diadem Urchin *(Diadema setosum)* which can be recognised by its long and very mobile spines. It is rarely visible during the day, but very frequently seen at night. It can assume colouring which varies from black to light grey, often with violet tones. Wounds from its spines are particularly painful, given that they penetrate deep into the flesh, breaking and making their extraction very difficult. The Slate-pencil Urchin *(Heterocentrotus mammillatus)* lives in shallow water where wave movement is particularly intense, and for this reason it has short thick spines which allow it to attach itself firmly to the rock. Its name comes from the fact that in the past the spines were used to write on blackboards.

305

Asteroidea (Starfish)

Starfish have an pleasing and amusing shape, often connected in our minds with strip cartoons or our childhood. In reality they are strong predators which must fill the molluscs and crustaceans on which they feed with terror. It is not, in fact, rare to turn over a starfish and find that it is intent on devouring a shellfish with a really extraordinary system. The stomach can in fact be everted so as to envelope prey much larger than the body of the starfish, which is quite small if the arms are excluded. Therefore digestion takes place outside until the powerful gastric juices have partially dissolved the calcareous structure of the prey, allowing the starfish to digest the organic part. In the case of bivalves, the arms of the starfish grip the shell and exert an extremely strong traction on the two valves until they open. A few years ago a starfish called Crown of Thorns *(Acanthaster planci)* because of the large number of spines which cover its surface, ended up in the newspapers. This starfish feeds on coral polyps and has undergone, for reasons which are still not clear, a sudden population explosion in some areas of the Pacific and in particular on the Australian Great Barrier Reef. Vast stretches of reef have been destroyed, without there having been found an effective method to check the irresistible advance.

306 - *Fromia sp.*
307 - *Culcita sp.*
308 - *Fromia elegans*
309 - **Pin-cushion Starfish** *(Choriaster granulosus)*
310 - *Fromia monilis*

306

307

308

309

310

311

312

313

REGENERATION OF STARFISH

*M*any starfish have an incredible regenerative capacity which allows them to re-form arms or any part of the body which is missing. The terrible Crown of Thorns (**Acanthaster planci**), for example, if cut in two, regenerates the missing part of its body after some time, causing even greater damage to the environment. This was observed with horror by the Australian divers who tried to kill these diabolic starfish underwater because they were destroying vast stretches of the Great Barrier Reef. **Linckia multifora**, a starfish which is very common in the Maldives, is however the master in the art of regeneration. If an arm is lost "in battle", after a short time another one starts growing. But that is not all, even the amputated arm can regenerate a whole new starfish and divers can observe the various growth stages of the new star which has an unusual "comet" shape. The longest arm is that which the original star was deprived of, whilst the short ones are the new arms which are forming. This technique is so effective that starfish also use it for reproducing asexually, voluntarily breaking off an arm which will make a new starfish.

311 - *Linckia multifora* in its characteristic "comet" form, as it regenerates the rest of its body from an arm.
312 - *Linckia multifora*
313 - *Linckia sp.*
314, 315 - Crown of Thorns (*Acanthaster planci*)

314

315

120

316

317

318

319

Holothuroidea (Sea cucumbers)

The shape of the *Holothuroidea* does not even vaguely resemble that of the other echinoderms, given that they are long and thick, rather like large cucumbers. They live on sandy and detrital sea beds, where they sift the sediment with their tentacles which encircle the mouth, searching for the little organisms on which they feed. Although filtering species are not lacking, most swallow large quantities of sand and are without a doubt one of the organisms which turn over the sand on the sea bed most. It has been calculated that the sea cucumbers present in a hectare are able to shift 150 tons of sand in a year. To defend themselves, many species use a very unusual system which consists of expelling a mass of fine white filaments which coagulate on contact with the water, becoming tremendously sticky. As a drastic solution they resort instead to the expulsion of their entrails, which then are slowly regenerated in the course of a few months. In the Orient, sea cucumbers are fished for food, boiled and then dried in the sun to be cooked as *Trepang*, a prized dish in Chinese cooking.

320

316 - Sea cucumbers
317 - *Holothuria edulis*
318, 319 - *Thelenota ananas*
320 - Striated Sea Cucumber *(Bohadschia graeffei)*
321 - *Stichopus variegatus*

321

322

TUNICATES -Ascidiacea (Sea squirts)

Sea squirts are seemingly very simple organisms, which in the solitary form look like a little sack with two openings. In reality they are very highly evolved organisms, which in their larval stage have a tail furnished with a notochord, that is, a kind of backbone, which systematically places them very high up in the evolutionary ladder. They are divided into solitary and colonial forms, the latter often being confused with sponges. On careful examination, however, the two openings which characterised each single individual can be distinguished. These two holes are nothing but an inhalent siphon, through which water is sucked into the organism, and an exhalent siphon from which water is expelled, once the plankton on which the sea squirt feeds has been retained. Sea squirts are hermaphrodite, but self-fertilization is not possible as the male and female reproductive organs in the same individual reach maturity at different times. Many species also reproduce asexually, thanks to their extraordinary regenerative powers, which allow the formation of a whole new individual from a little particle of the ''donor''.

323

322 - Clavelinids
323, 326 - *Didemnum molle*
324 - Sea squirts
325 - *Didemnum sp.*

324

GENERAL INDEX

332

CETACEA

An encounter with cetaceans is quite frequent in the Maldives, particularly if one takes a cruise which allows one to reach the more remote atolls. In the stretches of open sea one mostly comes across the smallish Striped Dolphins of the *Stenella sp.* They like to come to ride on the bow wave of boats and sometimes assemble in groups of a large number. Inside the lagoons, on the other hand, an encounter with the Bottlenosed Dolphin *(Tursiops truncatus)* is more likely. This dolphin is larger, being able to reach over three metres in length and is characterised by a darker grey colouring on its back. Its face is well known to everybody, as these are the classic dolphins that can be seen in dolphinariums and have been the stars of a long series of television programmes. Encounters with *Grampus griseus* are also not rare; it is easily recognised by its slate grey colouring crossed through by extensive "scratches" of a lighter colour. These grampuses can reach 4 metres in length and prefer deep waters, but sometimes approach the reef near the passes where there is a greater concentration of fish on which they feed.

333

332, 333 - Striped Dolphins *(Stenella longirostris)*

with rhythmic strokes, its body tilting slightly backwards. When frightened, they are capable of considerable acceleration, outstriping a diver with no difficulty, but inevitably succumbing to more hydrodynamic predators. These are made up almost entirely of certain sharks, principally the Tiger Shark, which is able to break up the carapace with its powerful jaws. Out of 400 Tiger Sharks captured, 350 had the remains of turtle in their stomach. These reptiles have adapted perfectly to a marine environment in the course of their evolutionary history, to the extent that they pass their whole life in the sea, apart from the females, that during the reproduction period must return to dry land to lay their eggs under the sand.

Their capacity for orientation is extraordinary: when the females reach sexual maturity they always return to lay their eggs on the very beach on which they were born, and the little turtles when just hatched, are capable of reaching the sea, attracted by its reflected light.

The most common species in the Maldives are the Common Turtle, the Green Turtle and the Imbricated Turtle.

329

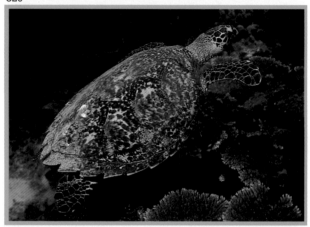

330

329, 331 - Green Turtle *(Chelonia mydas)*
330 - Imbricated Turtle *(Eretmochelys imbricata)*

331

TURTLES

Turtles have always been hunted in the Maldives, though the government is trying to limit their commerce. Turtle meat is eaten as a good alternative to fish, the oil is used to treat lung problems or in cosmetics and the carapace to produce jewelry and objects which are prized in all countries. These things are regularly displayed and sold in every Maldivian village but the purchase of them is prohibited and commerce should not be in any way encouraged, in order to avoid accelerating the extermination of these wonderful reptiles. Seeing a turtle swimming underwater is one of the most thrilling encounters for a diver. Using its powerful forelimbs, the turtle proceeds

327 - *Caretta caretta*
328 - Imbricated Turtle
    (*Eretmochelys imbricata*)

327

328

325

326